The Complete Guide to
Painting on
Porcelain & Ceramic

Priscilla Hauser

Sterling Publishing Co., Inc.
New York

Prolific Impressions Production Staff:

Editor in Chief: Mickey Baskett
Copy Editor: Ellen Glass
Graphics: Dianne Miller, Karen Turpin
Styling: Lenos Key
Photography: Jerry Mucklow
Administration: Jim Baskett

Every effort has been made to ensure that the information presented is accurate. Since we have no control over physical conditions, individual skills, or chosen tools and products, the publisher disclaims any liability for injuries, losses, untoward results, or any other damages which may result from the use of the information in this book. Thoroughly read the instructions for all products used to complete the projects in this book, paying particular attention to all cautions and warnings shown for that product to ensure their proper and safe use.

Library of Congress Cataloging-in-Publication Data

Hauser, Priscilla.
 The complete guide to painting on porcelain and ceramic / Priscilla Hauser.
   p. cm.
 Includes index.
 ISBN-13: 978-1-4027-3988-0
 ISBN-10: 1-4027-3988-5
 1. China painting. I. Title.

NK4605.H39 2007
738.1'5--dc22

2007005950

2 4 6 8 10 9 7 5 3 1

Published by Sterling Publishing Co., Inc.
387 Park Avenue South, New York, NY 10016
©2007 by Prolific Impressions, Inc.
Distributed in Canada by Sterling Publishing
c/o Canadian Manda Group, 165 Dufferin Street,
Toronto, Ontario, Canada M6K 3H6
Distributed in the United Kingdom by GMC Distribution Services,
Castle Place, 166 High Street, Lewes, East Sussex, England BN7 1XU
Distributed in Australia by Capricorn Link (Australia) Pty. Ltd.
P.O. Box 704, Windsor, NSW 2756, Australia

Printed in China
All rights reserved

ISBN-13: 978-1-4027-3988-0
ISBN-10: 1-4027-3988-5

For information about custom editions, special sales, premium and corporate purchases, please contact Sterling Special Sales Department at 800-805-5489 or specialsales@sterlingpub.com.

Acknowledgements

A special thanks to Sue Sensintaffar, Collette Ralston, Judy Kimball, Barbara Saunders, and Janet Alphin, who all helped with the development and painting of these projects and instructions.

Thank you to the following manufacturers for supplying the products to complete the projects in this book.

For the Robert Simmons Sienna line of brushes: Daler-Rowney, (800-278-1783) www.daler-rowney.com

For FolkArt® Enamels™ paints: Plaid Enterprises, Inc., www.plaidonline.com

For Sta-Wet Artist Palette: Masterson Art Supply, www.mastersonart.com

Thanks to Tony Tanner for colored porcelain pieces: Black Iris Studios, Inc., 8005 w. 48th Ave., Denver CO., www.blackirisstudios.com

For white china such as the cake plate, rectangular birthday boxes, and place settings: Dallas China, Inc., 8428 Hwy. 121 North, Melissa, TX 75454, www.dallaschina.com

For white china pieces such as round birthday box and ginger jar canister: Rynne China Company, 222 West Eight Mile Rd., Hazel Park, MI 48030, www.rynnechina.com

About the Artist

Priscilla Hauser

She's the "First Lady of Decorative Painting," and with good reason. Due to Priscilla's efforts, dreams, and ability to draw people to her, the first meeting of the National Society of Tole & Decorative Painters took place on October 22, 1972, with 21 other people attending. Since then the organization has thrived, and so has Priscilla.

From Priscilla's beginning efforts as a tole painter in the early 1960s, having taken tole painting classes at a YMCA in Raytown, Missouri, she has become a world renowned teacher, author, and the decorative

painting industry's ambassador to the world. She has used nearly every outlet to share her enthusiasm for and knowledge of decorative painting. Besides teaching all over the world, Priscilla has illustrated her technique through books, magazine articles, videos, and television. The results of her teaching method have led to an accreditation program for teachers. She has traveled to teach in Canada, Japan, Argentina, and The Netherlands, as well as extensive teaching within the United States at her "Studio by the Sea" in Panama City Beach, Florida.

For information about Priscilla Hauser Painting Seminars,
you can contact Priscilla as follows:
Priscilla Hauser
P.O. Box 521013, Tulsa, OK 74152
Fax: (918) 743-5075
Phone: (918) 743-6072
Website: www.priscillahuaser.com
email: phauser376@aol.com

TABLE OF

CONTENTS

PAGE 83

PAGE 109

PAGE 115

Painting on porcelain, ceramic and glass surfaces of all kinds used to be a bit of a
challenge. Years ago I used to china paint – you know, the type of painting that you
fire in a kiln. I loved it, but at that time there weren't any automatic kilns. I would
forget to watch the cones, and melt all of my china. That wasn't fun. It also wasn't fun
to paint and fire, paint and fire, paint and fire to get the exciting colors I desired.

I still think china painting is beautiful, but when I found acrylic enamel
paints on the market – that didn't have to be fired, I simply flipped! (This isn't
a commercial.) I could layer the paint, let it dry 30 minutes between coats,
and that had the effect of a firing. I could get gorgeous effects similar to
china painting in much less time and with a great deal of ease.

*Wow, what a book! More flowers,
more pieces, more fun than perhaps
we have ever had went into
creating this wonderful book.*

The entire experience of painting on porcelain, china, or glass of any kind is
absolutely delightful. You can create pieces that you, your friends, and your family
will cherish for the rest of your lives. That is, if you don't drop them and break them.

To make painting on porcelain even more fun, I have discovered that colored
porcelain is now available. I love painting on this colored porcelain because no
background painting is necessary to get a smooth, dramatic colored background.
One of my favorites in this book is the white lilies on the gorgeous coral vase.

Whatever your favorite may be, get busy and start painting. You're
going to fall in love with what you do. You will see the hours fly by
so quickly, you'll hardly be able to believe it!

PAINTS
for Glass and Ceramic Surfaces

Acrylic Enamels

You can find a variety of products for painting on glass and ceramics. They all have assets and liabilities, but I have found that the acrylic enamels that can be heat set in your home oven work best for most of my purposes.

Acrylic enamels are easy to use paints that are a unique polymer blend specially formulated for use on glass and glazed ceramics. They are highly pigmented for excellent coverage. Choose paints that are waterbased and non-toxic. You can achieve a durable, opaque, glossy sheen with these paints, and there is no primer or finish needed. The paints can be mixed and blended. They clean up easily with soap and water.

Pieces painted with acrylic enamels can be air dried to cure in 21 days, or you can bake them in your home oven for added durability. Check the manufacturer's instructions on the label to be sure. The usual procedure is to put the painted pieces into a cold oven, heat it to 350 degrees, then bake for 30 minutes, turn off the oven, and let the pieces cool completely without touching them. The cured or baked pieces are waterproof and top-shelf dishwasher safe. Never allow a painted piece to soak in water, and do not use strong or abrasive cleaners.

Acrylic enamels are non-toxic. But, to be safe, manufacturers of acrylic enamel paints recommend that the paints not come in contact with food. Keep the painting about 3/4" away from the lip of a cup or glass. When painting on plates simply cover them with a clear glass dish for serving or eating food – they make wonderful chargers. When painting on a tray, cover the painted tray with clear plastic wrap before placing food. Or apply paint only to the edge of a plate.

Mediums for Acrylic Enamels

Do not thin acrylic enamels with water. Always use the painting mediums specifically formulated for the paint you're using. Mediums are liquids or gels that are mixed with paint for achieving specific effects. They are sold along with acrylic paints. It is best to use mediums and paints from the same manufacturer.

Clear medium gives paint a transparent quality, and thins the paint so it can be used for floating a color.

Flow medium helps paint flow off the brush, so it's helpful when painting line work or details.

Extender works like a blending medium. It gives the paint more open time, so you have more time to work the paint before it dries.

HINTS FROM PRISCILLA

- Acrylic paints like to be cold. They won't dry as quickly if the room temperature is 68 degrees or colder. Heat dries, cold does not.
- Do not allow air to blow on your project while you're painting. Rapidly moving air dries the paint. Still air allows you more time to move the paint.
- Humidity keeps things wet. The higher the humidity, the more time you'll have for blending.
- Use a lot of paint so the colors will blend together.

CERAMICS & PORCELAIN

The wonderful thing about the acrylic enamels is that they create beautiful effects on glazed and unglazed ceramics as well as on glass. Today there are many pieces available for you to paint, from tiny china boxes to dramatically large floor vases.

Porcelain

Porcelain is made from three different materials: kaolin, a very pure white clay; feldspar, ground-up quartz rock; and flint, which causes the kaolin and feldspar to blend together during firing into a translucent ceramic body. Their proportions determine the firing temperature, which can range from 2300 degrees F (1260 degrees C) to over 3000 degrees F (1649 degrees C).

Glazed Porcelain:

Glaze is basically silica that melts into a clear solid surface when heated. Colored glazes are made of frit (ground-up glaze that has already been fired) mixed with water and chemicals that yield specific colors when fired. For example, cobalt fires blue and copper gives greens or reds depending on the temperature. Porcelain pieces are glazed when still in the greenware or unfired stage. The glaze and the clay are fired all at one time.

To prepare glazed porcelain for painting, wash the piece with soap and water, rinse thoroughly, and dry. Wipe the surface with rubbing alcohol to remove any traces of oil or detergent residue.

Porcelain Bisque:

"Bisque" refers to clay pieces that are fired without glaze. Porcelain bisque is simply a porcelain clay piece that has been completely fired to the mature stage without any glaze. It is hard and non-porous; it will hold water without any glazing inside the piece.

A bisque surface has some "tooth" to it. You may need to sand the surface lightly with fine sandpaper to make it smooth enough to paint. Wash, rinse, and dry, then wipe with rubbing alcohol.

Glazed China

While "china" originally meant "porcelain from China," it now refers to ceramic or earthenware pieces as well. Within the United States, regular ceramic pieces are fired to the bisque stage, glazed, and fired again to mature the glaze.

To prepare glazed china for painting, wash the piece with soap and water, rinse thoroughly, and dry. Wipe the surface with rubbing alcohol to remove any traces of oil or detergent residue.

Glass

While glazes create a hard, smooth surface very like glass, glass has a different makeup. Glass pieces are available everywhere, in an infinite variety of sizes and shapes. Simply wash, rinse, and dry, then wipe with rubbing alcohol and you're ready to paint.

BRUSHES

When it comes to brushes, please purchase the very best that money can buy. They are your tools – the things you paint with. Occasionally, a student says, "Priscilla, I don't want to buy a good brush until I know I can paint." I always tell my students they won't be able to paint if they don't begin with a good brush. You get what you pay for.

There are many different types of brushes, and different-shaped brushes do different things. Choose brushes that are meant for painting on ceramics and porcelain. The hair of these brushes is a bit softer, which helps to lay the paint on the slick china in a smooth way.

The size brush you will use at any given time depends upon the size of the area you are painting. Small designs require small brushes, medium designs require medium brushes, and large designs require large brushes. Trying to paint without the proper size brush is a major mistake. *Here's a Tip:* Wear a head band binocular magnifier when using your smallest brushes to paint tiny areas.

You will need four types of brushes in various sizes. Individual project instructions list the types and sizes of brushes needed for that particular project.

Flat Brushes

Flat brushes are designed for brush strokes and blending. These brushes do most of the painting of the designs. Sizes used in this book are flats #0 through #20. You will also need a 1" wash brush.

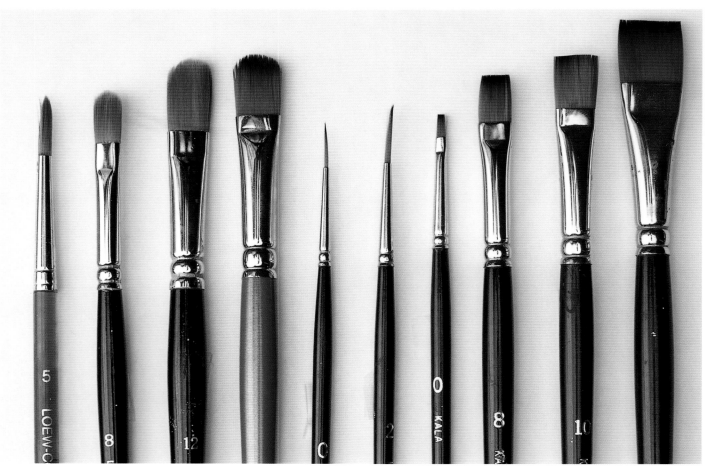

Brush types, pictured left to right: Round, filbert, liner, flat.

Round Brushes

Round brushes are used primarily for stroking – we seldom blend with them. They can also be used for some detail work. The size used in this book is #5.

Filbert Brushes

Filbert brushes are a cross between a flat and a round brush. They are generally used for stroking, but can also be used for blending. Sizes used in this book are #2, #4, #6.

Liner Brushes

Liner brushes are very thin round brushes that come to a wonderful point. Good liner brushes are needed for fine line work. Sizes used in this book are #1, #10/0.

Other Paint Applicators

Sponges give textural interest when they are used to dab paint onto a surface. Kitchen sponges give a more open texture, sea sponges are finer, and make-up sponges are finest of all.

A **toothbrush** is the perfect tool for spattering thinned paint in a spray of tiny dots.

Sponge brushes can be used for basecoating large areas.

Stencil brushes can be used to pounce or dab paint on surfaces.

Sponge daubers are these round sponges on the end of a stick. They are great for painting circular design motifs – you can find them in a variety of sizes.

You may also use your **fingers** to rub paint onto the rim of a vase or the edge of a lid.

BRUSH CARE

It's important to clean your brushes properly and keep them in excellent condition. To clean them thoroughly:

1. Gently flip-flop each brush back and forth in water until all the paint is removed, rinsing them thoroughly. Never slam brushes into a container and stir them.
2. Work brush cleaner through the hairs of the brush in a small dish and wipe the brush on a soft, absorbent rag. Continue cleaning until there is no trace of color on the rag.
3. Shape the brush with your fingers and store it so nothing can distort the shape of the hairs. Rinse the brush in water before using again.

Pictured above: Sponge dauber for circular design motifs.

BASIC PAINTING SUPPLIES

In addition to paint, mediums, and brushes, these are the basic painting supplies you will need for each project. They are not listed in the individual project instructions; you will, however, need to gather them for each and every project.

Tracing Paper – I like to use a very thin, transparent tracing paper for tracing designs. I use a **pencil** for tracing.

Graphite Transfer Paper – I use wax free, white or gray graphite paper to transfer my design.

Stylus – I use a stylus tool for transferring the traced design to the prepared surface. A pencil or a ballpoint pen that no longer writes also may be used.

Palette – I like to use a "stay-wet" type palette system. Some people prefer a wax-coated or dry palette for acrylics; however, I prefer a palette that stays wet since acrylics dry so quickly. A wet palette consists of a plastic tray that holds a wet sponge. Also included with this palette system is a special palette paper. This paper should be soaked overnight and then placed on top of the wet sponge. Wipe the surface of the paper with a soft, absorbent rag to blot any excess water. When using enamels, dampen the sponge and wring out excess water so it is almost dry. Place the paper on top of the semi-wet sponge. Water is not a friend of the enamels. If too much water mixes with the paints, they will not adhere properly to the china surface or to each other. Therefore, you want to use the wet palette to keep the paints from drying, but you don't want too much water. It's like adjusting your oven to the proper temperature for baking. Palettes can be found where decorative painting supplies are sold.

Palette Knife – Use a palette knife for mixing and moving paint on your palette or mixing surface. I prefer a straight-blade palette knife made of flexible steel.

100% Cotton Rags – Use only 100% cotton rags for wiping your brush. *Try the knuckle test: For 15 seconds, rub your knuckles on the rag that you wipe your brush on. If your knuckles bleed, think of what that rag is doing to the hairs of your brush!* You could also use soft, absorbent **paper towels** for wiping brushes.

Water Basin – Use a water basin or other container filled with water for rinsing brushes.

Brush Cleaner – Clean your brushes thoroughly after each painting session.

Rubbing Alcohol – Wipe the clean, dry surface of your glass or ceramic piece with alcohol to remove traces of grease, detergent residue, or oils from your skin. All of these can prevent the bonding of the acrylic enamels to the surface. After wiping with alcohol, avoid touching the surface with your hands.

Fine Sandpaper – Sand the surfaces of porcelain bisque pieces lightly, if needed to get a smooth surface for painting.

Transferring Patterns

Transferring a Design with Transfer Paper

See Photo 1.

1. Trace the pattern neatly and carefully from the book on tracing paper, using a pencil or fine point marker.
2. Position tracing on surface. Secure with tape.
3. Slide the transfer paper under the tracing with the transfer side facing the surface.
4. Using a stylus, neatly trace over the pattern lines to transfer the lines to the surface.

Photo 1

Transferring with Chalk

See Photos 2 & 3.

If you choose a piece of pre-colored porcelain that is dark, you can transfer your design to the surface with white chalk. Or if you choose to paint the surface background with a dark color, you can use this technique.

1. Neatly trace the pattern of the design onto tracing paper. You may use a pencil or a pen. It's not necessary to trace shading lines or curlicues.
2. Turn over the traced design. Firmly go over the traced lines on the back with chalk. Do not "scribble" over the entire back of the tracing, simply trace over the lines.
3. Shake off the excess chalk dust, being careful not to inhale the particles

4. Position the design on the prepared surface, chalk side down. Tape in place if necessary.
5. Using a stylus, go over the lines. Chalk is easily removed and it dissolves as you paint over it.

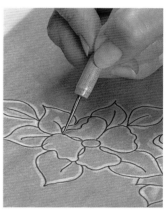

Photo 2 *Photo 3*

Transferring a Design with Charcoal Pencil

See Photos 4 & 5.

1. Neatly trace the pattern of the design onto tracing paper. You may use a pencil or a pen.
2. Turn over the traced design. Firmly go over the traced lines on the back with a charcoal pencil.
3. Position the design on the prepared surface, charcoal side down. Tape down with masking tape if needed.
4. Using a stylus, go over the lines. The pattern line will be transferred to your surface.

Photo 4 *Photo 5*

Learn and Practice Brush Strokes

Brush strokes are the basis of my decorative painting technique. This book includes excellent brush stroke worksheets for practicing. To use them, lay a sheet of acetate or tracing paper over the top of the worksheet, choose a brush approximately the same size as the brush used on the worksheet, and practice hundreds of strokes on top of mine. (If a hundred sounds like a lot, get over it! You will find that painting a hundred strokes happens very quickly.)

Painting a Solid Color Background

A piece of white porcelain can be entirely painted with enamels to create a solidly colored background.
1. Wash with soap and water, let dry.
2. Wipe with alcohol, let dry.
3. Using a wide brush in good condition, stroke the enamel evenly on the surface of the china. Be generous with the amount of paint you are using and use a light touch as you apply the paint. Additional coats may be applied, but allow the paint to dry 30 minutes between coats.

Preparing the Wet Palette

A wet palette consists of a plastic tray that holds a wet sponge and special paper. To use this type of palette:

1. Soak the sponge in water until saturated. Wring out. Place the sponge into the tray. (**Photo 1**)

2. Soak the paper that comes with the palette in water for 12-24 hours. Place the paper on top of the very wet sponge. (**Photo 2**)

3. Wipe the surface of the paper with a soft, absorbent rag to remove the excess water. (**Photo 3**)

4. When paints are placed on top of a properly prepared wet palette (**Photo 4**), they will stay wet for a long time.

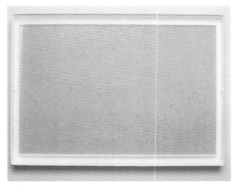

Photo 1

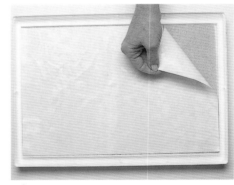

Photo 2

Photo 3

Photo 4

Using a Round Brush

Round brushes are used primarily for stroking – we seldom blend with them. They come in a variety of sizes. Practice your round brush strokes on the Brush Stroke Worksheets.

Loading the Brush

Photo 1. Squeeze paint on your palette. If needed, thin your paint with flow medium. Paint should be a creamy consistency.

Photo 2. Load brush by picking up paint from the edge of the puddle.

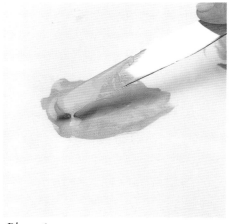

Photo 1

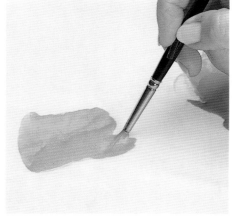

Photo 2

Teardrop or Polliwog Stroke

Photo 1. Touch on the tip of the brush and apply pressure.

Photo 2. Gradually lift and drag straight down. Turning the brush slightly left or right forces the hairs back together to form a point.

Photo 1

Photo 2

Comma Stroke – Left

Photo 1. Angle the tip of the brush toward the left corner of the practice page. Touch on the tip of the brush and apply pressure.

Photo 2. Begin lifting and pulling to the inside edge of the brush, dragging until a point is formed.

Comma Stroke – Right

This stroke is done the same way as the left comma stroke, but the tip of the brush is angled toward the right corner of the practice page.

Photo 1

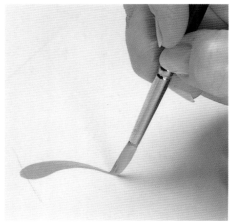

Photo 2

Using a Filbert Brush

The filbert is a variation of the round brush, and it is used in much the same way.
Notice that the stroke looks slightly different with a filbert brush.

Comma Stroke – Left

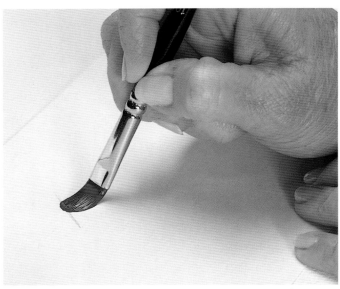

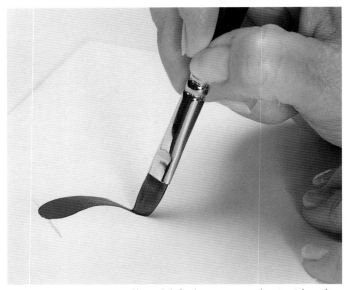

Photo 1. Angle the tip of the brush toward the left corner of the practice page. Touch and apply pressure.

Photo 2. Begin to pull and lift, leaning to the inside edge of the brush. Drag to a point.

Comma Stroke – Right

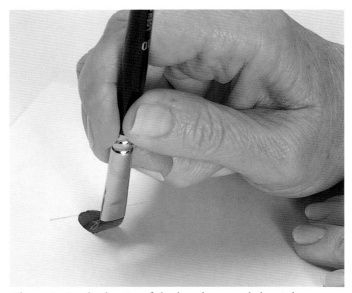

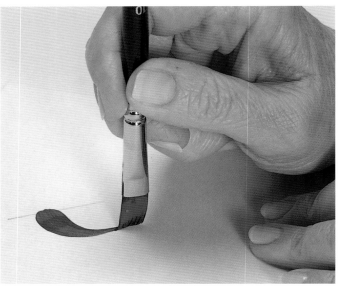

Photo 1. Angle the tip of the brush toward the right corner of the practice page. Touch and apply pressure.

Photo 2. Pull the brush. Begin lifting and pulling to the inside edge of the brush, dragging it until a point is formed.

Using a Flat Brush

Flat brushes are designed for brush strokes and blending. They come in many different sizes. Flat brush strokes or any type of stroke may be painted in a single color. It is always a good idea to practice the stroke using a single color before you double-load. These photos show a double-loaded brush, but the procedure is the same if you are using a single color. Practice your flat brush strokes on the Brush Stroke Worksheets.

Double-Loading

Double-loading involves loading your brush with two colors. Be sure to thin the paint with medium to a flowing consistency and push it with a palette knife to form a neat puddle with a clean edge.

Photo 1. Stroke up against the edge of the light color 30 times, so half of the brush is loaded with paint and the other half is clean.

Photo 2. Turn the brush over and stroke up against the edge of the dark color 20 times.

Photo 3. Blend, blend, blend one side of the brush on your palette.

Photo 4. Turn the brush over and blend, blend, blend on the other side, keeping the dark color in the center and the light color to the outside.

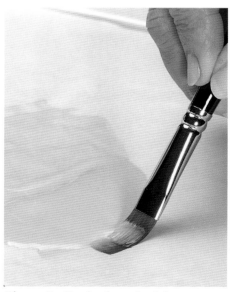

Photo 5. Go back and pick up more light paint on the brush.

Photo 6. Go back to the blending spot on your palette and blend some more.

continued on next page

Double Loading, continued

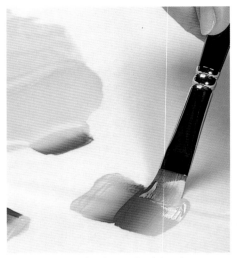

Photo 7. Go back and pick up some more dark color.

Photo 8. Go back to the blending spot on your palette and blend some more. Continue doing this until your brush is full.

Photo 9. Here is a correctly double-loaded brush. You don't want a space between the two colors; you want them to blend together.

Line Stroke

1. Stand the brush on its flat (chisel) edge, perpendicular to the orientation of the basic flat stroke. The handle should point straight up.
2. Pull the brush toward you. Don't press the brush down, as this will thicken and distort the line.

Basic Stroke

1. Touch the flat (chisel) edge of the brush to your surface.
2. Press the brush down and pull it toward you, holding the pressure steady. Lift the brush smoothly at the end of the stroke.

Comma Stroke

1. Touch the flat (chisel) edge of the brush at an angle to the left corner of the practice page. *Tip: Drawing the roof of a house with a pencil when you practice may help you find the correct angle.*
2. Press down and pull the brush, then lift the brush gradually back up to its flat edge as you pull it to the left. Don't pick up the brush too quickly, or hold the pressure too long.
3. Drag to a point.

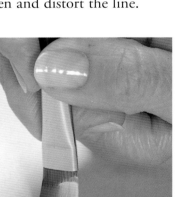

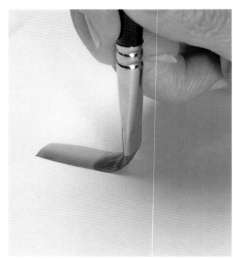

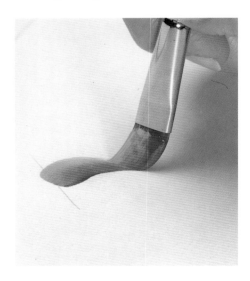

Comma Stroke Right

To angle a comma stroke in the opposite direction, touch the brush at an angle to the right corner of the practice page. Press down and pull the brush, then lift the brush gradually back up to its flat edge as you pull it to the right and drag to a point.

S-Stroke Left

1. Stand the brush on the flat (chisel) edge, angled to the left corner of the practice page, with the handle pointing straight up.
2. Pull, letting the brush roll to the left. Gradually apply pressure.
3. Pull, lifting slowly back up to the flat (chisel) edge at the end of the stroke.

S-Stroke Right

This stroke can be reversed for a right S-stroke.

Tip: Use a pencil to draw S-strokes as a guide. Do your practice strokes over the pencil marks, keeping the pencil line in the middle of your brush stroke.

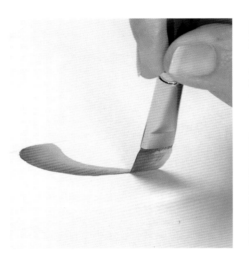

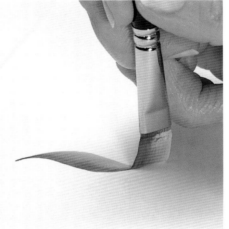

U-Stroke

1. Touch the brush on the flat (chisel) edge with the handle pointing straight up.
2. Pull the brush toward you, gradually applying pressure.
3. Lift the brush away from you just as gradually, back to the flat edge. This stroke can be reversed for an upside-down U-stroke.

Half-Circle Stroke

1. Touch the brush on the flat (chisel) edge. Press the brush down.
2. Holding the pressure steady, pivot or roll the brush so that you create a half circle.
3. Lift. *Note: This is the only time the flag on your brush should wave, as you deliberately pivot the brush in this stroke.*

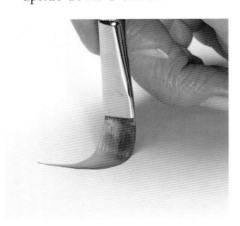

Using a Liner Brush

Liner brushes are the long, thinner members of the round brush family. Their bristles come to a wonderful point. Liner brushes are used for fine line work. Practice your liner brush strokes on the Brush Stroke Worksheets.

Loading the Brush

Photo 1. Thin paint with flow medium until it is the consistency of ink.

Photo 2. Fill the brush full of paint by pulling it through the paint edge. Twist the brush as you pull it out of the puddle; this will form a nice pointed tip. When you are using the brush hold it straight up.

Teardrop Stroke

Photo 1. Fill brush with paint of a thin consistency; touch, apply pressure.

Photo 2. Begin pulling and lifting.

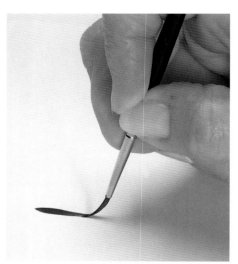

Photo 3. Drag to a point.

Comma Stroke – Angled Left

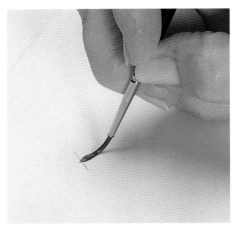 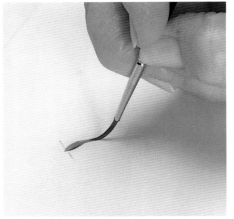 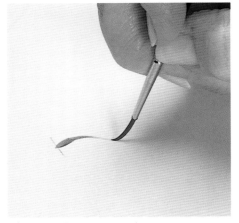

Photo 1. Angle the brush toward the left corner of the practice page. Touch and apply pressure.

Photo 2. Begin to pull and lift, leaning to the inside edge of the brush.

Photo 3. Drag to a point.

Comma Stroke – Angled Right

1. Angle the brush toward the right corner of the practice page. Touch and apply pressure.
2. Begin to pull and lift, leaning to the inside edge of the brush.
3. Drag to a point.

TIPS FROM PRISCILLA

- Be sure you have a good brush in excellent condition.

- Thin the paint with the proper medium to an almost ink-like consistency.

Curlicues & Squiggles

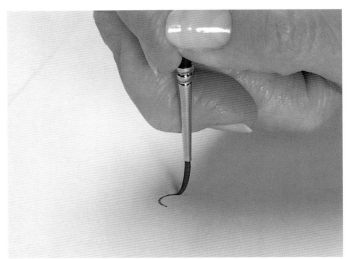 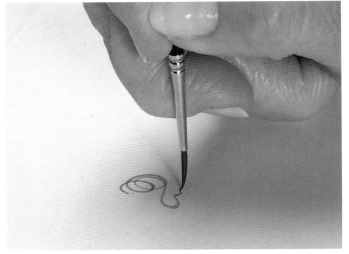

Photo 1. Stand the brush on its point with the handle pointing straight up toward the ceiling.

Photo 2. Slowly move the brush to paint loopy M's and W's. Practice several times on your page. Make as many variations as you wish.

BRUSH STROKE WORKSHEET

Round Brush Strokes

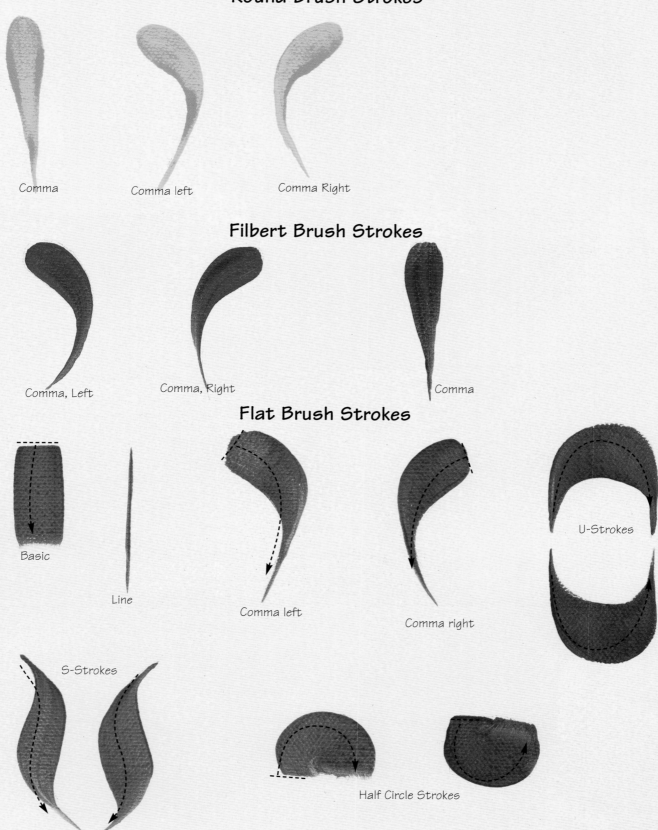

Comma

Comma left

Comma Right

Filbert Brush Strokes

Comma, Left

Comma, Right

Comma

Flat Brush Strokes

Basic

Line

Comma left

Comma right

U-Strokes

S-Strokes

Half Circle Strokes

BRUSH STROKE WORKSHEET

Double-Loaded Brush Strokes (using a #12 flat brush)

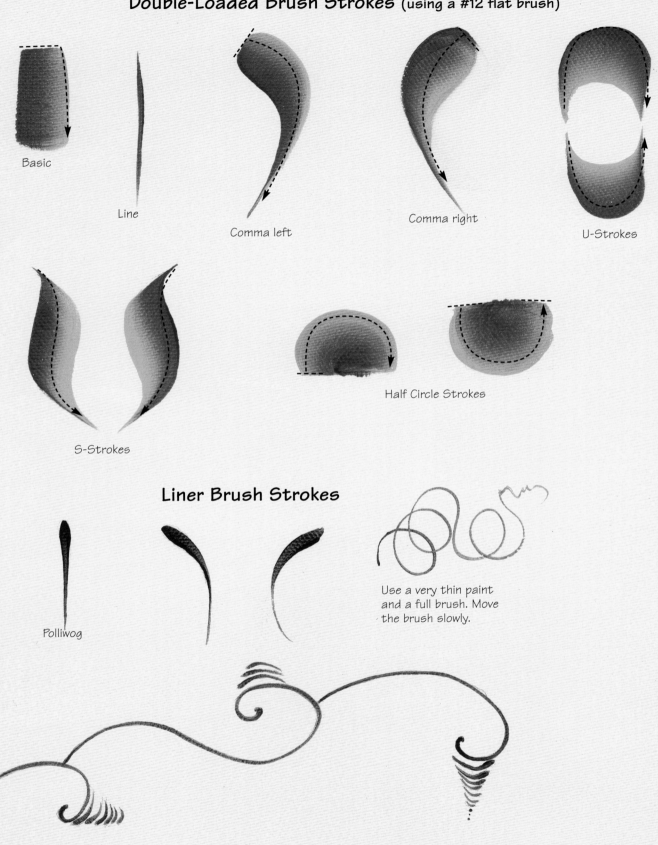

Basic

Line

Comma left

Comma right

U-Strokes

S-Strokes

Half Circle Strokes

Liner Brush Strokes

Polliwog

Use a very thin paint and a full brush. Move the brush slowly.

Floating Technique

Floating is flowing color on a surface. This technique is used for adding the shading and highlighting to design elements. Before floating, basecoat the design area. For example, if you are painting a leaf, solidly paint the leaf area with the medium tone of leaf color. Let dry. Add a second or even a third coat, if necessary. Let dry. Our example shows shading and highlighting floated on a leaf that has been basecoated in a gray-green color.

Note: If I am painting on a very dark area, I may undercoat the design area first with white paint. I allow this to dry, then I basecoat with the medium tone of paint used to paint the leaf or flower.

Photo 1. Fill your brush with flow medium or clear medium. Use the largest brush possible for the size of the design area you are painting.

Photo 2. Fill one side of the brush with the shading color by stroking up against the edge of a puddle of paint.

Photo 3. On a matte surface, such as tracing paper or wet palette paper, blend, blend, blend on one side of the brush.

Photo 4. Then turn the brush over and blend, blend, blend on the other side. Keep the paint in the center. Be sure the brush is good and full of paint and that the color graduates through the brush from dark to medium to clear.

Photo 1

Photo 2

Photo 3

Photo 4

Photo 5. The floating of shading and highlighting will be done on top of the basecoating. Here the leaf was basecoated with Fresh Foliage, a soft green color.

Photo 6. Float on the shading to the edge of the design (leaf), with the dark side of the brush toward the outside of the design. Let dry. Repeat the process, if desired, to deepen the color.

Photo 7. Highlighting is floated on the opposite side of the design. Rinse the brush, blot dry, and load with flow medium and the light color. Use the same blending technique. Keep the light color side of the brush toward the edge of the design while floating the highlight.

Blending Technique

In this book, I have done a very easy type of blending. First, neatly and carefully basecoat the design element and let it dry. Extender, which slows drying and allows you to easily blend colors together, is painted onto the design area that you want to blend. Work quickly through all the blending steps while the extender remains wet. When you have finished blending, allow the layer of blended paint to dry for 20 to 30 minutes, just as you would dry a coat of a single color.

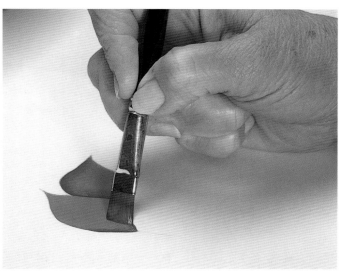

Photo 1. Float on the shadows. Let dry.

Photo 2. Add a small amount of extender medium to the area of design where you will be blending color.

Photo 3. Add the colors you wish to blend on top of the wet medium.

Photo 4. Lightly blend or move the colors together, using an extremely light touch. If you are heavy handed, you will wipe all the color away. If this happens, let the extender dry and cure at least 30 minutes and begin again, *or* remove the color before it dries, add more extender, and begin again.

CREATIVE TECHNIQUES

There are many fun, often quick and easy techniques that can be used to
make backgrounds, to add finishing touches, or to create a design on a surface.
Often, when I finish a piece, I'll study it carefully, then add spattering or sponging.
Sometimes I embellish the piece with dots, dashes, and line work that really
make a finished piece smile. Any of these techniques can be combined with
the design patterns to give them your own unique, creative touch.

Spattering

Another term for spattering is flyspecking. I use this technique a lot to
add a finished, relaxed look to a painted design. My favorite way of spattering uses a medium- or soft-bristled toothbrush.

1. Thin the paint with flow medium to a thin consistency.
2. Rub the toothbrush in the paint. *Photo 1*
3. Pull your thumb toward you over the bristles and watch the different size
   specks fall to the surface. Practice on a piece of paper until you can control this technique. *Photo 2*

Photo 1

Photo 2

*Pictured left: This ginger-jar canister is
spattered with the green colors used to
paint the ivy that twines around it.
Instructions are on page 122.*

Stenciling a Design

Stenciling can be quick and easy. You can purchase ready made stencils
in hobby and craft stores or online, or you can cut your own.

Supplies needed for cutting your own stencil:

Clear acetate or frosted plastic (such as Mylar®)

Permanent marker

Piece of glass to use as a work surface while cutting

A cutting tool of your choice – sharp scissors, a rotating craft knife, or the stencil point of a hot knife tool.

Supplies needed for stenciling:

Stencil of your choice

Masking tape or stencil adhesive

Stencil brush or sponge dauber

Paper towels

Acrylic enamel paints

How to stencil:

1. Trace your design onto the acetate. Using your cutting tool of choice, carefully cut out the stencil.

2. Tape the stencil in place on clean surface or secure it with spray-on stencil adhesive.

3. Load the brush by pouncing on the palette. Rub the brush onto a clean paper towel, leaving very little paint in the brush. *Photo 1*

4. Pat or pounce the paint through the stencil onto the surface. *Photo 2* Let dry. Repeat as needed. Carefully remove the stencil and wash it before storing.

Butterflies & Moths: The butterfly and moth design was stenciled onto tinted clear glass. Use a pre-cut stencil or cut your own from the pattern on page 124. Charcoal paint was used for the bodies and French Blue and Deep Lilac for the wings.

Photo 1

Photo 2

Background Sponging

Different types of sponges create different looks on backgrounds. A sea sponge gives a more mottled look, but a fine make-up sponge can give a blended background. An ordinary kitchen sponge can often add just the creative touch you are looking for.

Supplies Needed:
Sponge of choice
Paint colors of choice
Tape for masking

Instructions:
1. Dip the sponge in water to soften it. Squeeze out as much water as possible.
2. Place the paint on the palette. Dab the sponge in the paint, pouncing the sponge up and down to load it. *Photo 1*
3. Using an up-and-down motion, sponge the paint onto the surface. *Photo 2*
4. If desired, a second color may be added. If you are using a second color, it may be applied while the first color is wet or you can wait until the first color has dried thoroughly. The effects are different; try both ways on a practice board. ❑

Photo 1

Photo 2

Dot Work

Dots are frequently used to create berries and flower centers, but they can be strong decorative elements on their own. Dots are fun to paint and can be done in many different ways. One of my favorite ways is to use a sponge-on-a-stick applicator (dauber) that comes in large and small sizes.

Using a Sponge Dauber

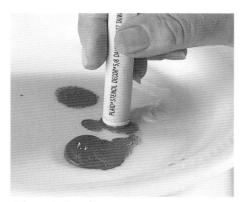

1. Dip the sponge applicator in water or in the medium of your choice. Blot on a rag or paper towel.
2. Thin the paint with flow medium to the consistency of heavy cream.
3. Fill the sponge applicator with paint. *Photo 1* Blot on the rag.
4. Touch to the surface, press, wiggle slightly, and lift straight up. *Photo 2*

Photo 1. Loading

Photo 2. Dotting

Photo 3. Using a large dauber.

Using a Brush Handle or Stylus

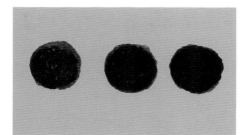

You can make small, medium, or large dots by varying the size of the brush handle or stylus and the amount of paint.

1. Thin the paint with flow medium to the consistency of ink.

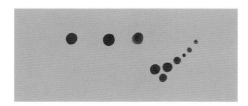

2. Dip the brush handle or stylus in the thin paint.

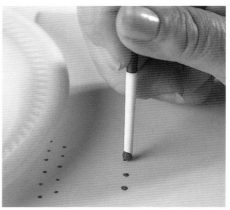

3. Touch to the surface, then lift straight up.

Dot Work, continued

Using a Liner Brush

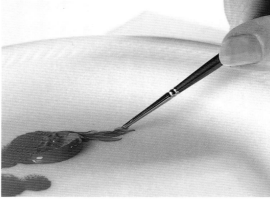

Photo 1. Loading

Photo 2. Dotting

Use a #1 liner brush in excellent condition that comes to a good point. Remember, the paint must be a thin, flowing consistency.

1. Rinse the brush in water. Blot on a rag.
2. Thin the paint with flow medium to the consistency of ink.
3. Dip the point in the paint. *Photo 1*
4. Touch to the surface to create the dots. Lift the brush straight up. *Photo 2*

Checks

Checks can be made in a number of different ways. You can paint checks with the width of the brush. You can create checks with masking tape. Checks can also be created with a stencil or with a square piece of sponge.

Checks with a Flat Brush

1. Make straight guide lines on your surface for the length of your check. The width of the check will be the width of your brush.
2. Load a flat brush with the color of your choice.
3. Put the chisel edge of the brush at the top guide line. Pull it down to the bottom guide line and lift. *Photo 1.*
4. Continue across surface, allowing a brush-width space between each stroke.
5. For next line, alternate the placement of the strokes. *Photo 2.*

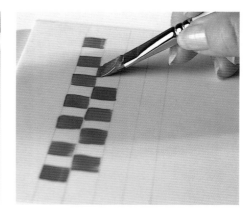

Checks by Masking

1. Choose a size of masking tape that you wish for the size of your checks.
2. Place a strip of tape horizontally across the area of the surface where you want your first row of checks. The tape should cover the length of the area where you want the checked row.
3. Place another strip of tape below the first strip where the second row of checks will be painted.
4. Continue placing strips of tape for as many rows of checks that you want. *Photo 1*
5. Now remove *every other* row of tape. *Photo 2*
6. Begin placing vertically rows of tape, each row next to the other. Place them across the area where you want your checks. *Photo 3*
7. Remove every other row of tape. *Photo 4*
8. Paint into the open square areas. *Photo 5*
9. Remove tape. *Photo 6*
10. When paint has dried (about an hour). Place rows of tape vertically and horizontally to cover the painted rows. This will leave open squares to create a checkerboard.
11. Paint into the open squares.
12. Remove tape.

Photo 1

Photo 2

Photo 3

Photo 4

Photo 5

Photo 6

Mottled Backgrounds

Mottling is a combination of sponging and washing. To create the mottled background on the vase painted with Larkspurs, pictured on page 83, I used a soft sea sponge with small holes and very thin paint. The effect is very subtle. You will need a sea sponge and a 1" wide wash brush.

1. Sponge project surface as explained in the "Background Sponging" technique instructions.
2. Make a wash by thinning the paint with flow medium to a very thin consistency.
3. Load the 1" wash brush with paint. *Photo 1.*
4. Apply the paint to the sponged background, pull paint across surface. *Photo 2.*

Photo 1

Photo 2

Shadowing Around the Design

This technique adds contrast and depth to the design. I usually do the shadowing with a dark color such as Payne's Gray or Burnt Umber.

1. Trace and transfer the design to your prepared surface.
2. Double load a large flat brush with flow medium and paint. Blend on the palette to soften, so that the color is shaded across the width of the brush from dark to light to clear.
3. Keeping the colored side of the brush against the outside of the design element, slowly apply the paint around the design, pulling the brush away from the design.

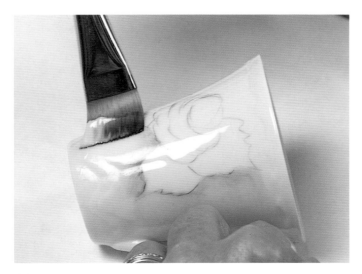

Adding Gold Edging

Rims on plates, trays and vases that won't come in contact with food look so beautiful when given a finishing touch of gold. Use metallic gold paint and a dauber to sponge the paint onto the rims.

Line Work

If you follow my exact directions for creating line work, you will find that you will do it beautifully. Keep these points in mind:

- Try not to drink caffeine before doing any line work!
- Use an excellent liner brush in excellent condition.
- Thin the paint to an ink-like consistency.
- Fill the brush good and full of paint. Be sure there is no medium on the ferrule of the brush.
- Be sure you can see the paint flow from the point of the brush. Your reading glasses are designed for reading, not for detailed painting or needlework. I use a binocular headband magnifier to do my line work.

1. **Prepare paint:** Thin the paint with flow medium until it is the consistency of ink. *Photo 1*
2. **Load the brush:** Pull the liner along the edge of the thinned paint until it is loaded. As you pull the brush out of the paint, twist it to a point. *Photo 2*
3. **Making a straight line:** With the brush on the tip, pull it along the surface to make a straight line. Painting straight lines take practice, just painting a line over and over again. The more pressure you put on the brush, the wider the line will be. If your lines aren't perfectly straight, don't worry about it. You want this to look hand painted; you certainly don't want it to look like a decal.
4. **Painting swirls:** When creating lines, curlicues, or swirls, move the brush slowly – don't go too fast. Keep the brush on the tip. Give the paint time to flow from the point of the brush to the surface. I say "liner" you say "thin." That's right ... always a thin consistency for line work. *Photo 3.*

Photo 1

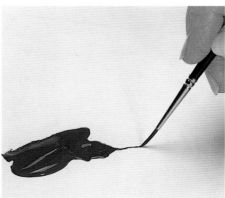

Photo 2

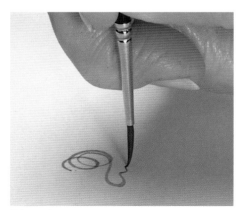

Photo 3

Stripes, Dots & Linework
Teapot & Cups

You'll find with dots and stripes that it is easy to create your own design, or you can trace and transfer the pattern on page 125. (Before you transfer the pattern, wash the pieces with soap and water, rinse, and dry thoroughly. Wipe surfaces with rubbing alcohol and let dry.) The painting is easy and the results are terrific. Have fun!

Brushes:

Use the largest brush size that is comfortable for you when painting each area. I used flat sizes #2, #4, #6, #8, and the #1 liner brush.

Acrylic Enamels Palette of Colors:

Burnt Umber

Butler Magenta

Evergreen

Fresh Foliage

Hydrangea

Lemon Custard

Purple Lilac

Wicker White

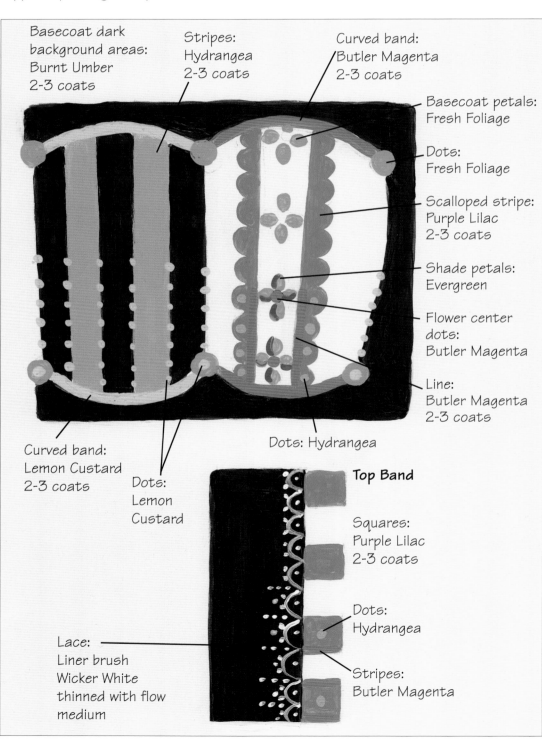

Basecoat dark background areas: Burnt Umber 2-3 coats

Stripes: Hydrangea 2-3 coats

Curved band: Butler Magenta 2-3 coats

Basecoat petals: Fresh Foliage

Dots: Fresh Foliage

Scalloped stripe: Purple Lilac 2-3 coats

Shade petals: Evergreen

Flower center dots: Butler Magenta

Line: Butler Magenta 2-3 coats

Curved band: Lemon Custard 2-3 coats

Dots: Lemon Custard

Dots: Hydrangea

Top Band

Squares: Purple Lilac 2-3 coats

Dots: Hydrangea

Stripes: Butler Magenta

Lace: Liner brush Wicker White thinned with flow medium

DESIGNS TO PAINT

Flowers of the Months

Flowers of the months are gorgeous to paint on any type of porcelain,
china, or glass. Throughout the following pages we have done just that.
Choose any surface. It's easy to modify a pattern to fit the piece you want
to paint. Simply trace the pattern and cut the tracing into pieces. Lay them on
the surface, and move them around as if you were solving a puzzle. You may
need to add a leaf or flower here and there, but you will find it is easy to do.
You can add words and lettering for a personal touch. It's easy to change sizes
by using a photocopier to enlarge or reduce the patterns. When you like the
arrangement, tape the pieces together, transfer your design, and go for it!
Patterns can come from a number of places, such as fabrics, wallpaper,
or even coloring books. Ideas can be found in magazines or mail order
catalogs. Of course, you must be aware of copyrights; do not
paint and sell anything that is already copyrighted.

Birthday Boxes

Pictured right

Is someone special having a birthday? Paint one of these small
china keepsake boxes with the flower of the month.

Violets for February – *Instructions are on page 46; pattern is on page 49.*

Red Roses for June – *Instructions are on page 78; pattern is on page 75.*

Yellow Roses for June – *Instructions are on page 79; pattern is on page 75.*

Carnations for January
Candle Lamp

This blue glass lampshade used with a candlestick is beautiful and unique. These types of candle holders and shades can be found at department stores and craft shops. These lamps are so versatile and so much fun to personalize to suit your décor and party theme.

Pattern on page 44

SUPPLIES

Acrylic Enamels:
Fresh Foliage
Green Forest
Lemon Custard
Midnight
Wicker White

Brushes:
Flats – #2, #4, #6
Liner – #1

Surfaces:
Blue glass lampshade
Glass candlestick

Other Supplies:
In addition to the basic painting supplies listed on page 14, you'll need:
Flow medium for acrylic enamels
Optional: Extender for acrylic enamels

INSTRUCTIONS

See the Carnations Painting Worksheet on pages 42 and 43 for detailed instructions for painting the flowers and leaves.

Prepare the Surfaces:
1. Wash the lampshade and candlestick with soap and water. Rinse and dry thoroughly.
2. Wipe the surfaces with rubbing alcohol. Let dry.
3. Neatly trace the design on tracing paper and transfer with wax-free transfer paper or chalk.

Paint the Design:

Use the brush size that best fits the area you are painting. Allow paint to dry 20 to 30 minutes between coats.

These carnations are painted on a dark background. By letting the background show through while using Wicker White to paint the petals with floating techniques, the background gives depth and shades the petals.

1. Paint the leaves as shown on the painting worksheets, using the colors and the brushes listed.
2. Paint the carnation petals and buds as shown on the painting worksheets.
3. Using the carnation colors, embellish the base of the candlestick with dots and comma strokes.

Finish:
Let the lampshade and candlestick air dry for 21 days *or* bake according to the paint manufacturer's instructions. ❑

Pictured left: Close-up of lamp base.

Carnations for January
Painting Worksheet

PALETTE OF COLORS

Fresh Foliage

Green Forest

Lemon Custard

Midnight

Wicker White

Figure 1

- Double load a #4 flat brush with flow medium and then Wicker White.
- Keeping the Wicker White to the outside, scribble with a back-and-forth motion to create outside edges of petals.

Figure 2

Continue with second and third rows of petals.

Basecoat stems and leaves with two or three coats of Fresh Foliage using the #2 flat brush.

Figure 3

Finish painting the rows of petals for entire flower.

Shade the left side of stem with a float of Green Forest, using the #2 flat brush.

Figure 4

Using the #1 liner brush, highlight and add comma stroke details to outside edges of petals with Wicker White.

Shade each petal in the shadow area with a float of Midnight.

Highlight the right side of stem with a mix of Lemon Custard + Fresh Foliage (1:1).

BUD

Figure 1

Basecoat with two or more coats of Fresh Foliage using the #2 flat.

Figure 2

Shade with a float of Green Forest using the #2 flat.

Figure 3

Highlight by floating a mix of Wicker White + Fresh Foliage (1:1).

LEAF & STEM

Figure 1

Basecoat with two or more coats of Fresh Foliage using the #6 flat.

Figure 2

Shade with a float of Green Forest.

Figure 3

Shade with a second and third float of Green Forest.

Figure 4

Highlight with a float of Wicker White + Lemon Custard (1:1).

Carnations for January

Patterns

Pattern for Candle Lamp

Actual Size

Bonus Patterns

Violets for February
Painting Worksheet

PALETTE OF COLORS

Autumn Leaves

Dioxazine Purple

Fresh Foliage

Lemon Custard

Magenta

Thicket

Warm White

Figure 1

Undercoat area of violet petals

Undercoat leaves

Background wash

Figure 2

Paint violets on top of the undercoating.

Dark background shading wash

Add shading and highlighting strokes to leaves.

Figure 3

Add lightest value violets.

Paint violet centers with liner brush.

Blend leaf while paint is still wet.

Violets for February
Round Porcelain Box

If blues and purples calm and relax you, you will enjoy painting these violets and leaves. This is a gorgeous box to celebrate a February — the month of love. It looks like fine kiln fired porcelain when you use the background mottling and shading technique.

SUPPLIES

Acrylic Enamels:

Autumn Leaves
Dioxazine Purple
Fresh Foliage
Lemon Custard
Magenta
Thicket
Warm White

Brushes:

Flats – #2, #4, #8, #10
Liner – #1
Wash brush – 1"

Surface:

Round porcelain powder box, soft blue, 6-1/2" diameter

Other Supplies:

In addition to the basic painting supplies listed on page 14, you'll need:
Flow medium for acrylic enamels
Extender for acrylic enamels
Clear medium for acrylic enamels

INSTRUCTIONS

See the Violets Painting Worksheet for detailed instructions for painting the flowers and leaves.

Prepare the Surface:

1. Wash the porcelain box and lid with soap and water. Rinse and dry thoroughly.
2. Wipe the surfaces with rubbing alcohol. Let dry.
3. Neatly trace the design on tracing paper and transfer with wax-free transfer paper.

Paint the Background Wash:

1. Double load the 1" wash brush with Dioxazine Purple and clear medium. Blend on the palette to soften the color. Float around the outside edge of the pattern outline. Let dry 20 to 30 minutes. *See Figure 1.*
2. Double load the 1" wash brush with Magenta and clear medium. Blend on the palette to soften the color. Add additional shadowing around the design. *See Figure 2.* Let dry.

Paint the Leaves:

Use the brush size that best fits the area you are painting. Allow paint to dry 20 to 30 minutes between coats.

1. Using a large #10 flat brush, base-coat leaves with two or three coats of Fresh Foliage. *See Figure 1.*
2. Apply a little extender to one leaf at a time. This will help blend colors on the leaf while the extender is wet.
3. Double load the #10 flat brush with Fresh Foliage and Thicket. Blend on palette to soften color. Stroke on dark side of leaf. *See Fig. 2.*

Continued on next page

Violets for February

Continued from page 47

4. Wipe the brush. Double load with Fresh Foliage and Warm White. Stroke on light side of leaf. *See Figure 2.*

5. Wipe the brush and lightly pull the brush in the direction of the strokes to blend the colors. *See Figure 3.*

Paint the Violets:

1. Using the #6 flat brush, undercoat violets with brush strokes of Dioxazine Purple. *See Figure 1.*

2. Using the #2 flat brush and a mix of Dioxazine Purple + Midnight, plus a touch of Warm White, stroke the five petals that create the violet. *See Figure 2.*

3. Using the #2 flat brush, pick up a little Warm White and stroke through a little Dioxazine Purple. You don't want the violets to look striped. Paint the lightest value violets, here and there. Be sure you can see the darker values underneath. *See Figure 3.*

4. Paint center details with the liner brush. Add Warm White comma strokes. Add a little Lemon Custard to the very center of the flower, stroking down onto the large lower petal. Dot Autumn Leaves at the very center with the liner brush. *See Figure 3.*

Curlicues:

Use the liner brush to paint curlicues with a mix of Thicket + Fresh Foliage, thinned with flow medium.

Finish:

Let the porcelain box and lid air dry for 21 days *or* bake according to the paint manufacturer's instructions. ❏

Pattern for Round
Porcelain Box

Actual Size

Pansies for February

Patterns

Instructions on page 52

Pattern for
Serving Plate

Actual Size

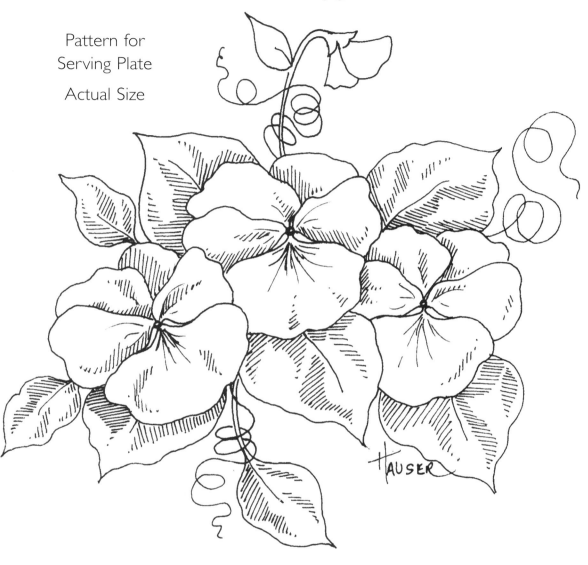

Pattern for Violets
Birthday Box

Actual Size

See page 39

Pansies for February
Painting Worksheet

PALETTE OF COLORS

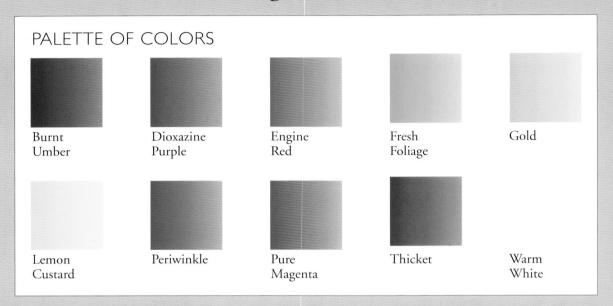

Burnt Umber	Dioxazine Purple	Engine Red	Fresh Foliage	Gold
Lemon Custard	Periwinkle	Pure Magenta	Thicket	Warm White

Figure 1
Undercoat with two coats of Periwinkle + Warm White (1:1).

Undercoat with two coats of Warm White.

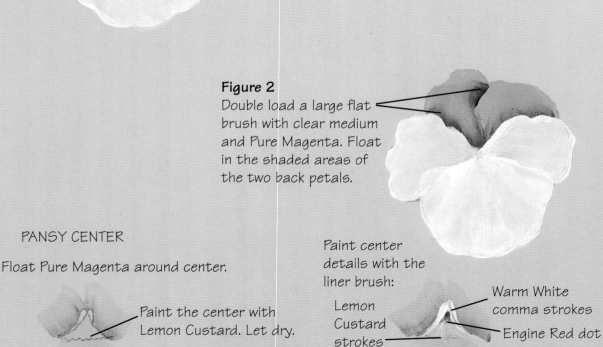

Figure 2
Double load a large flat brush with clear medium and Pure Magenta. Float in the shaded areas of the two back petals.

Paint center details with the liner brush:

Lemon Custard strokes

Warm White comma strokes

Engine Red dot

PANSY CENTER

Float Pure Magenta around center.

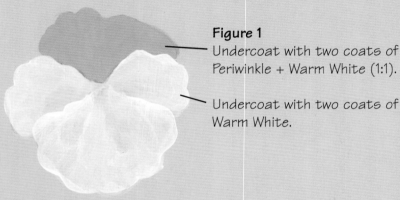

Paint the center with Lemon Custard. Let dry.

Figure 3

Float Dioxazine Purple on the two back petals.

Float Pure Magenta on the three front petals.

Figure 4

Shade with Dioxazine Purple + Pure Magenta (1:1). Blend. Float a second coat of Pure Magenta on the three front petals. Apply a coat of extender to the back petals.

Add more Warm White highlights if desired.

Color Option

Paint back petals Warm White. Shade with Pure Magenta + Dioxazine Purple (3:1).

Deepen shading on back petals with Pure Magenta + Dioxazine Purple (2:1).

Paint front petals Periwinkle. Shade with Pure Magenta + Dioxazine Purple (1:1).

PANSY BUD

Figure 1

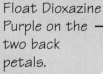

Undercoat petals with two or three coats of Periwinkle + Warm White (1:2).

Figure 2

Undercoat stem with two coats of Fresh Foliage.

Shade petals with Pure Magenta.

Highlight petals with Warm White.

Figure 3

Shade stem with Burnt Umber.

Highlight stem with Warm White.

Pansies for February
Serving Plate

This would make a wonderful plate for a special friend's birthday.
It would be beautiful as a tray on a dressing table or entry, as a piece
of art, or it can be used as a very special serving piece. If using it to serve,
be sure that food does not come in contact with the paint — use
a clear glass plate on top of painting or a plastic or paper doily.

Pattern on page 49.

SUPPLIES

Acrylic Enamels:

Burnt Umber

Dioxazine Purple

Engine Red

Fresh Foliage

Gold Metallic

Lemon Custard

Periwinkle

Thicket

Warm White

Brushes:

Flats – #4, #8, #10, #12

Liner – #1

Filbert – #6

Surface:

Porcelain plate, 9" square

Other Supplies:

*In addition to the Basic Painting
Supplies listed on page 14,
you'll need:*

Clear medium

Flow medium

Sponge dauber

INSTRUCTIONS

Prepare the Surface:
1. Wash the china tray with soap and water. Rinse and dry thoroughly.
2. Wipe the surface with rubbing alcohol. Let dry.
3. Neatly trace the design on tracing paper and transfer with gray wax-free transfer paper.

Paint the Background Wash:
1. Make a mix of Pure Magenta and Thicket (1:1, or to your liking). Double load the 1" wash brush with the mix on one side and clear medium on the other. Blend on the palette to soften the color. Float the color around the outside edge of the design. Let dry 30 minutes.
2. Float again to deepen the color, if desired. Let dry.

Paint the Design:
Use the brush size that best fits the area you are painting. Allow paint to dry 20 to 30 minutes between coats.
1. Paint the leaves first, following the procedure shown on page 46. After the blended leaf has dried, deepen shading with double-loaded Burnt Umber and flow medium.
2. Paint the pansies as shown on pages 50 and 51.

Finish:
1. Trim the edge of the tray with Gold, patted on with a sponge dauber or your finger.
2. Let the tray air dry for 21 days *or* bake according to the paint manufacturer's instructions.
3. Do not allow food to touch the painted surface. To use for serving food, place a clear glass plate on top of the painted design. ❏

Use a dauber and metallic gold paint to sponge a beautiful finishing touch to the rim of your plate.

Iris for March
Night Light

The little painted night light makes a very special gift to "light the way" during those dark cold months of March. Iris are beginning to feel the warmth of the earth and pop from their bulbs.

SUPPLIES

Acrylic Enamels:

Dioxazine Purple

Fresh Foliage

Lemon Custard

Pure Orange

Thicket

Wicker White

Brushes:

Flats – #4, #6, #8, #10, #12

Liner – #1

Surface:

Night light with glass shade (Different styles can be found in hardware stores or housewares sections of department stores.)

Other Supplies:

In addition to the basic painting supplies listed on page 14, you'll need:

Flow medium for acrylic enamels

Optional: Extender for acrylic enamels

INSTRUCTIONS

See the Iris Painting Worksheet for detailed instructions for painting the flowers and leaves.

Prepare the Surface:
1. Wash the glass shade with soap and water. Rinse and dry thoroughly.
2. Wipe the surface with rubbing alcohol. Let dry.
3. Neatly trace the design on tracing paper and transfer with white wax-free transfer paper.

Paint the Leaves:
Use the brush size that best fits the area you are painting. Allow paint to dry 20 to 30 minutes between coats.
1. Paint the leaves first. Basecoat the leaves with two or three coats of Fresh Foliage. *See Fig. 1.*
2. Shade the leaves with a float of Thicket. *See Fig. 2.*
3. Shade the leaves a second time with a float of Thicket. *See Fig. 3.*
4. Paint stems with Fresh Foliage, then shade with Thicket. Highlight with Wicker White. *See Fig. 4.*
5. Add veins in the leaves with a liner brush and a mixture of Lemon Custard and Wicker White (1:1).

Paint the Iris:
1. Neatly basecoat the iris with 2 or 3 coats of Lemon Custard. *See Fig. 1.*
2. Shade the petals with Pure Orange which has been thinned with a touch of Flow Medium. *See Fig. 2.*
3. Paint the inside petal Pure Orange. *See Fig. 2.*
4. Make a mixture of Pure Orange and Dioxazine Purple (1:1). Shade the inside petal with this dark mixture. *See Fig. 3.*
5. Highlight the edges of the petals with Wicker White. *See Fig. 3.*
6. Using a liner brush paint the detail lines on the petals with a dark mixture of Pure Orange and Dioxazine Purple. *See Fig. 4.*

7. Paint the beard on the iris with the dark mixture. Highlight it with white. *See Fig. 4.*

Finish:
Let the glass shade air dry for 21 days *or* bake according to the paint manufacturer's instructions. ❑

Iris for March
Painting Worksheet

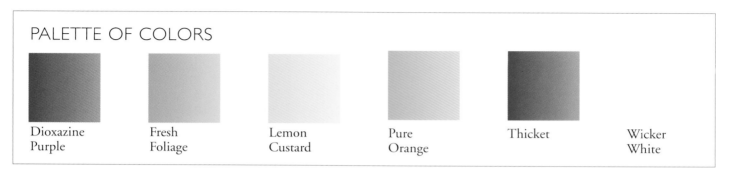

PALETTE OF COLORS

Dioxazine Purple   Fresh Foliage   Lemon Custard   Pure Orange   Thicket   Wicker White

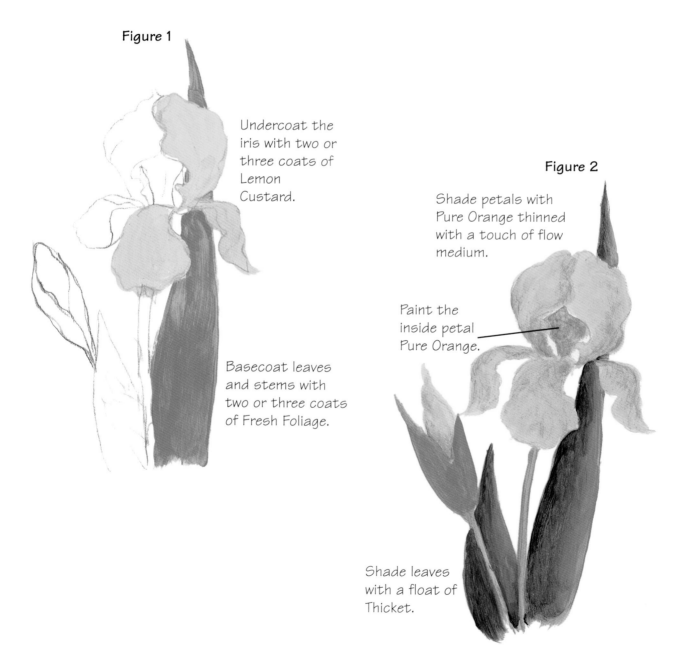

Figure 1

Undercoat the iris with two or three coats of Lemon Custard.

Basecoat leaves and stems with two or three coats of Fresh Foliage.

Figure 2

Shade petals with Pure Orange thinned with a touch of flow medium.

Paint the inside petal Pure Orange.

Shade leaves with a float of Thicket.

Figure 3

Shade the inside petal with a dark mix of Pure Orange + Dioxazine Purple (1:1).

Highlight edges of petals with Wicker White.

Deepen shading on leaves with a float of Thicket.

Figure 4

Using the liner brush, paint detail lines with the dark mix of Pure Orange + Dioxazine Purple (1:1).

Paint the iris beard with the dark mixture. Let dry. Highlight the beard with Wicker White.

Shade stems with Thicket. Highlight stems with Wicker White.

Using the liner brush, paint leaf veins with a mix of Lemon Custard + Wicker White (1:1).

Pattern for Night Light

Actual Size

Sweet Peas for April
Kerosene Lamp

I remember helping my grandmother plant the sweet pea seeds next to the fence each year. In the spring, those beautiful flowers would climb the fence and create the dearest blossoms. To me sweet peas are old fashioned and extremely nostalgic.

SUPPLIES

Acrylic Enamels:

Berry Wine

Engine Red

Fresh Foliage

Thicket

Wicker White

Brushes:

Flats – #4, #8, #10, #12

Liner – #1

Surface:

Round kerosene lamp base

Other Supplies:

In addition to the basic painting supplies listed on page 14, you'll need:

Flow medium for acrylic enamels

Extender for acrylic enamels

Clear medium for acrylic enamels

Sea sponge

INSTRUCTIONS

See the Sweet Peas Painting Worksheet for detailed instructions for painting the flowers and leaves.

Prepare the Surface:

1. Wash the lamp base with soap and water. Rinse and dry thoroughly.
2. Wipe the surface with rubbing alcohol. Let dry.
3. Neatly trace the design on tracing paper and transfer with wax-free transfer paper.

Sponge the Background:

1. Dip the sponge in water to soften it. Squeeze out the water.
2. Dip the sponge in clear medium and blot on a rag. Pick up a little Fresh Foliage and blot on a rag. Stipple or sponge the Fresh Foliage on the background as desired. Let dry.

Paint the Design:

Use the brush size that best fits the area you are painting. Allow paint to dry 20 to 30 minutes between coats.

1. Mix generous amounts of these two colors:
   Light Pink – Wicker White + a tiny touch of Engine Red. Use to basecoat blossoms.
   Dark Pink – Wicker White + Engine Red (4:1). Use for shading blossoms.
2. Paint the sweet peas as shown on pages 60 and 61.
3. Use the liner brush to paint curlicues with a mix of Thicket + Fresh Foliage, thinned with flow medium.

Finish:

Let the lamp base air dry for 21 days *or* bake according to the paint manufacturer's instructions. ❑

Sweet Peas for April
Painting Worksheet

PALETTE OF COLORS

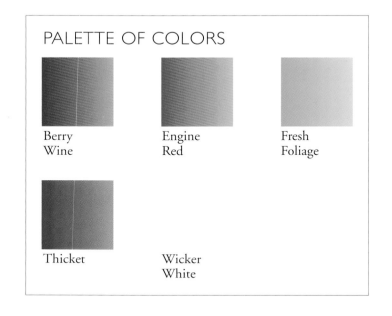

Berry
Wine

Engine
Red

Fresh
Foliage

Thicket

Wicker
White

Figure 1

Basecoat blossoms with two to three coats of the
Light Pink mix.

Basecoat stems and leaves with two
to three coats of Fresh Foliage.

Pattern for Lamp – Enlarge @ 130% for actual size

Figure 2

Double load a large flat brush with the Dark Pink mix and flow medium. Float shading on petals.

Shade stems and leaves with a float of Thicket.

Figure 3

Apply a little extender to one petal at a time.

While the extender is wet, apply a little Wicker White to the outside petals here and there. Pull the Wicker White into the extender to add highlights.

Figure 4

Apply extender again to one petal at a time.

While the extender is wet, shade with a little Berry Wine.

With the liner brush, add veins and highlights to the leaves and stems with a mixture of Wicker White + a tiny touch of Fresh Foliage.

Lilies for May
Porcelain Vase

White lilies are stunning on the coral background of this vase. This piece has lots of contrast, which is very different from the traditional look of china painting. No shading behind or around the design is needed when painting on dark colors. It's definitely more contemporary. I love it!

SUPPLIES

Acrylic Enamels:

Burnt Sienna

Fresh Foliage

Metallic Gold

Lemon Custard

Pure Orange

Thicket

Warm White

Brushes:

Flats – #10, #12, #16, #20

Liner – #1

Surface:

Large classic porcelain vase, coral, 12"

Other Supplies:

In addition to the basic painting supplies listed on page 14, you'll need:

Flow medium for acrylic enamels

Extender for acrylic enamels

Toothbrush

Optional: Small dauber

INSTRUCTIONS

See the Lilies Painting Worksheet for detailed instructions for painting the flowers and leaves.

Prepare the Surface:
1. Wash the vase with soap and water. Rinse and dry thoroughly.
2. Wipe the surface with rubbing alcohol. Let dry.
3. Neatly trace the design on tracing paper. Transfer with wax-free transfer paper.

Paint the Design:
To minimize brush strokes, use the largest brush that is comfortable in any area of the design. Allow paint to dry 20 to 30 minutes between coats.
1. Paint the leaves of the flower first. Paint them following the figures on the Painting Worksheet.
2. Paint the lilies next, following the figures on the Painting Worksheet.
3. Trim the top rim of the vase with Metallic Gold, rubbing it on with your finger or applying with the dauber. If using a dauber, use an up-and-down pouncing motion.

Finish:
Let the vase air dry for 21 days *or* bake according to the paint manufacturer's instructions. ❏

PAINTING ON COLORED PORCELAIN

I love painting on brightly colored porcelain. It gives such a richness to the design. However, you must be sure to undercoat your design with several coats of white paint before adding the basecoat, shading and highlighting colors. If you can't find the color porcelain you want, you can paint a plain white piece with the acrylic enamel paints. Be sure to let the piece dry thoroughly for several days before adding your painted design.

Lilies for May
Painting Worksheet

PALETTE OF COLORS

| Burnt Sienna | Fresh Foliage | Metallic Gold | Lemon Custard | Pure Orange | Thicket | Warm White |

Figure 1

Undercoat petals, bud, and leaves with three coats of Warm White.

Paint the bud with two or more coats of Fresh Foliage.

Figure 2

Shade lily petals with a float of Thicket where they join in the center. Let dry.

Float a second coat of Thicket to deepen the color.

Shade the bud with a float of Thicket. Let dry. Apply a second and third coat to deepen the shading.

Figure 3

Double load a large flat brush with Lemon Custard and flow medium. Float over the Thicket in the center of the flower.

Use the liner brush to paint stamens with Fresh Foliage thinned with flow medium.

Use the liner brush to paint the pollen with Pure Orange. Shade with a touch of Burnt Sienna.

Thin a little Thicket with flow medium. Load a toothbrush with this mix. Speckle the lilies' centers and petals.

LEAVES

Figure 1

Undercoat with three coats of Warm White.

Shade dark side of leaves with a float of Thicket.

Figure 2

Double load a large flat brush with Fresh Foliage and Thicket. Keeping the Thicket to the left, paint each leaf. Let dry.

Repeat two or three times. Let dry 20 to 30 minutes between coats.

Figure 3

Double load a large flat brush with Fresh Foliage and Warm White. Highlight leaves on the right side.

Repeat if desired, drying between coats.

Lilies for May

Patterns
Pattern for Vase
Actual Size

Roses for June
Porcelain Plate

I adore painting on the colored porcelain. The romantic pink roses make the little Bavarian dish one of my favorites. Since this is a very light colored background, shading around the rose design gives the design more depth.

SUPPLIES

Acrylic Enamels:

Berry Wine

Burnt Umber

Fresh Foliage

Thicket

Warm White

Wicker White

Brushes:

Flats – #2, #4, #20

Liner – #1

Surface:

Round Bavarian dish, dusty rose, 7-1/2" diameter

Other Supplies:

In addition to the basic painting supplies listed on page 14, you'll need:

Flow medium for acrylic enamels

Extender for acrylic enamels

INSTRUCTIONS

See the Traditional Pink Rose Painting Worksheet for detailed instructions for painting the flowers and leaves.

Pattern for Plate
Actual Size

Prepare the Surface:

1. Wash the dish with soap and water. Rinse and dry thoroughly.
2. Wipe the surface with rubbing alcohol. Let dry.
3. Neatly trace the design on tracing paper and transfer with wax-free transfer paper.

Paint the Design:

Use the brush size that best fits the area you are painting. Allow paint to dry 20 to 30 minutes between coats.

1. Paint the shaded background around the traced rose design first. Double

load the #20 flat brush with flow medium and a little Berry Wine. Blend on palette to soften color. Float around the outside edges of the design. *See Fig. 1.*

2. Paint the leaves before you paint the roses. Paint leaves as shown on Painting Worksheet. Because the leaves are under the roses, the rose petals will overlap the leaves.

3. Paint the roses as shown on Painting Worksheet.
4. Paint curlicues with the liner brush and Thicket thinned with flow medium.

Finish:

Let the dish air dry for 21 days *or* bake according to the paint manufacturer's instructions. ❏

69

Roses for June
Traditional Pink Rose Painting Worksheet

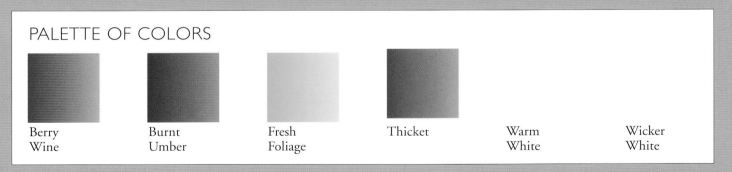

PALETTE OF COLORS

Berry Wine   Burnt Umber   Fresh Foliage   Thicket   Warm White   Wicker White

The roses in the step-by-step demonstration are larger than the roses on the porcelain dish so that you can easily see the process.

Figure 1

Double load the #20 flat brush with flow medium and a little Berry Wine. Blend on palette to soften color. Float around the outside edges of the design.

Figure 2

Double load the #20 flat brush with flow medium and a little Thicket. Blend on palette to soften color. Float Thicket here and there, over the Berry Wine.

Basecoat rose with Berry Wine.

Basecoat leaves with two or three coats of Fresh Foliage.

Figure 3

Apply a second and third coat of Berry Wine to rose.

Shade base of leaf with a float of Burnt Umber.

Figure 4

Double load the brush with Berry Wine and Wicker White or Warm White. Blend on palette to soften color. With the white to the outside edge of the petals, apply strokes 1, 2, and 3.

Float Thicket over the Burnt Umber.

Figure 5

Paint strokes 4, 5, 6, and 7.

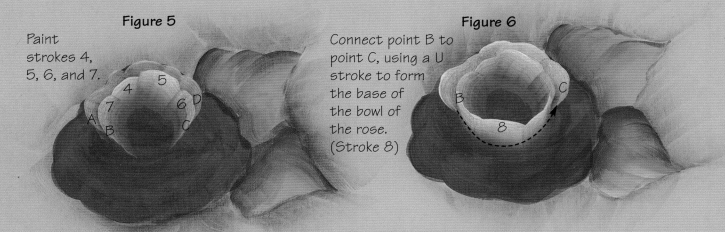

Apply a little extender to the leaf. Double load the brush with Fresh Foliage and Thicket. Paint the shadow and dark strokes. Continue with Figures 5 and 6 while the extender is wet.

Figure 6

Connect point B to point C, using a U stroke to form the base of the bowl of the rose. (Stroke 8)

Double load the brush with Fresh Foliage and Warm White. Stroke on the light side of the leaf.

Figure 7

Keeping the white to the outside edge of the petals, use comma strokes to paint petals 9, 10, 11, 12, and 13.

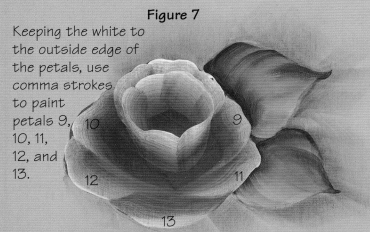

Quickly blend the colors. Add more of any color, if desired. Let dry.

Figure 8

Connect point A to point D with a U stroke. (Stroke 14)

If needed, repaint, darken, or lighten the leaves

Figure 10

Scalloped strokes

To finish the rose, add rolled S strokes and more comma strokes, creating petals.

Figure 9

Create petals over or on top of 9, 10, 11, 12 and 13. (Stroke 15 and 16)

Fill in the center with scalloped strokes.

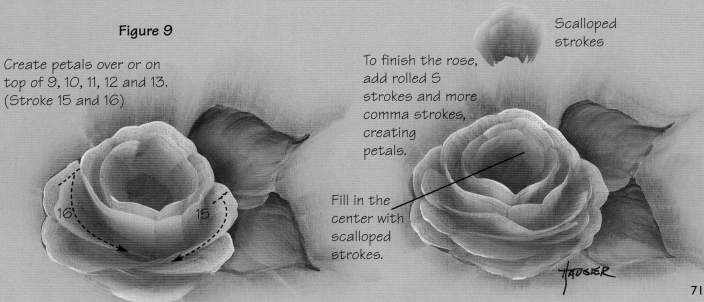

Hauser

Roses for June
Rosebuds Vase

Creating stripes is a fun and easy technique, and adds a bit of interest
to a background. Because the shape of the vase swells, the stripes
are wider at the top than at the bottom. The stripes provide
a beautiful contrast for the twining vines and curlicues.

SUPPLIES

Acrylic Enamels:
Autumn Leaves
Fresh Foliage
Lemon Custard
Skintone
Thicket
Warm White

Brushes:
Flats – #2, #4, #6
Liner – #1

Surface:
Porcelain oriental vase, peach, 6"

Other Supplies:
In addition to the basic painting supplies listed on page 14, you'll need:
Flow medium for acrylic enamels
Extender for acrylic enamels
Small dauber
Painters' tape, 1/4"
Fine sandpaper

INSTRUCTIONS

See the Rosebuds Painting Worksheet for detailed instructions for painting the flowers and leaves.

Prepare the Surface:
1. Sand the porcelain if needed with fine sandpaper.
2. Wash the vase with soap and water. Rinse and dry thoroughly.
3. Wipe the surface with rubbing alcohol. Let dry.

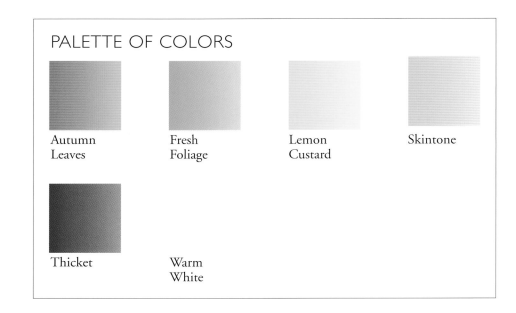

PALETTE OF COLORS

Autumn Leaves

Fresh Foliage

Lemon Custard

Skintone

Thicket

Warm White

4. Neatly trace the design on tracing paper and transfer with wax-free transfer paper.

Paint the Stripes and Rim:
1. "Eyeballing" the placement of the stripes works well. Start at the bottom and apply a strip of tape upward. Move over a little and apply another piece of tape. Move over that same amount and keep going all the way around.
2. Mix Skintone with flow medium to a thin consistency. Using a large flat brush, wash on the spaces between the tape. Don't use a lot of paint; you don't want it to bleed under the tape. If it does bleed, clean it up carefully with a little alcohol.
3. Mix a generous amount of coral mix: Warm White + Autumn Leaves (3:1). (This mix will also be used to paint the rosebuds.) Trim the top rim of the vase, using the dauber in an up-and-down motion.

Paint the Design:
Use the brush size that best fits the area you are painting. Allow paint to dry 20 to 30 minutes between coats.
1. Paint the leaves first. Paint leaves as shown on Painting Worksheet.
2. Paint the rosebuds as shown on Painting Worksheet.
3. Paint the bracts last as shown on Painting Worksheet.

Finish:
Let the vase air dry for 21 days *or* bake according to the paint manufacturer's instructions. ❏

Roses for June
Rosebuds Painting Worksheet

Paint the rosebuds before you paint the bracts, since the bracts overlap the buds.

CLOSED BUD

Figure 1
Basecoat rosebud with two or three coats of the coral mix.

Basecoat bracts, bases of the buds, and stems with two or three coats of Fresh Foliage.

Figure 2
Double load a large flat brush with the coral mix and Autumn Leaves. Blend on palette to soften color. Shade the base of the bud.

Figure 3
Deepen the shading with a second coat.

Double load a small flat brush with Fresh Foliage and Thicket. Shade bracts and stem.

Figure 4
Float Warm White on bracts and stems to highlight the edges.

Figure 5

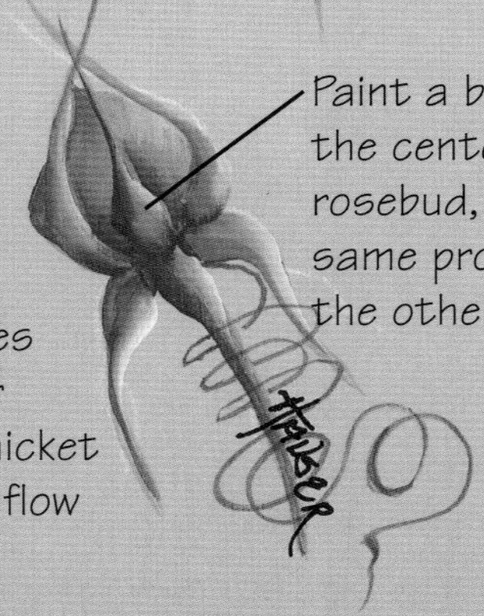

Paint a bract up over the center of the rosebud, following the same procedures as the other bracts.

Paint curlicues with the liner brush and Thicket thinned with flow medium.

OPEN BUD

Figure 1
Basecoat rosebud with two or three coats of coral mix.

Basecoat bracts, bases of the buds, and stems with two or three coats of Fresh Foliage.

Figure 2

Apply a dot of Autumn Leaves in the center of the bud.

Double load the brush with Autumn Leaves and the coral mix. Blend on palette to soften color. Paint a U stroke from left to right. Repeat several times so the color shades from dark to medium to light.

Shade bracts and stem with a float of Thicket.

Note: Left-handed painters will find it easier to stroke from right to left.

Figure 3

Highlight bracts and stem with Warm White.

Thin Warm White with flow medium. Place dots to create the white flowers, using the point of the liner brush, a stylus, or a paintbrush handle.

Double load the brush with Autumn Leaves and the coral mix. Blend on palette to soften color. Paint a U stroke to form the bowl of the rose. Let dry. Repeat as many times as desired to deepen the color.

Figure 4
Paint a bract up over the center of the rosebud to enclose it, following the same procedures as the other bracts.

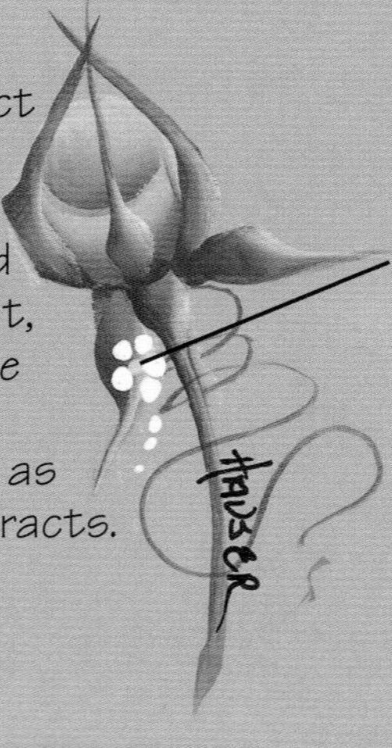

Thin Lemon Custard with flow medium. Dot the centers of the white flowers.

Paint curlicues with the liner brush and Thicket thinned with flow medium.

Pattern for Vase
Enlarge @130% for actual size.

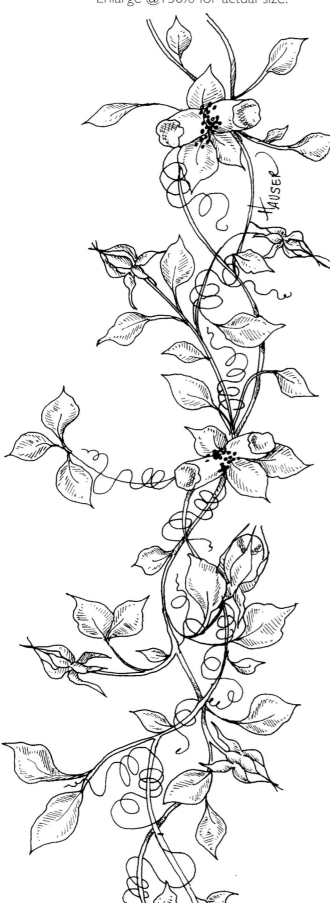

Roses for June
Patterns

Pattern for Red Roses Birthday Box
Actual Size

Pattern for Yellow Roses Birthday Box
Actual Size

Instructions for Birthday Boxes begin on page 78.

PALETTE OF COLORS

 Berry Wine

 Dioxazine Purple

 Engine Red

 Fresh Foliage

 Pure Orange

 Thicket

Warm White

The roses in the step-by-step demonstration are much larger than the roses on the birthday box so that you can easily see the process.

Mix these colors for the roses. By varying the mixes, you can make the roses as light or dark as you like.

Red mix:
Engine Red + Pure Orange (1:1)

Light mix:
Warm White + Engine Red + Pure Orange (3:1:1)

Dark mix:
Berry Wine + a touch of Dioxazine Purple

Figure 1

Basecoat rose with red mix.

Basecoat leaves with two or three coats of Fresh Foliage.

Figure 2

Apply a second and third coat of the red mix to the rose.

Shade base of leaf with a float of Thicket + a touch of Burnt Umbe

Figure 3

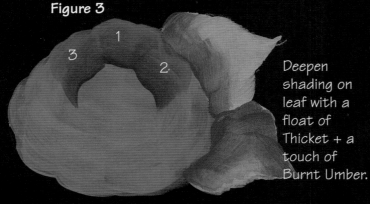

Deepen shading on leaf with a float of Thicket + a touch of Burnt Umber.

Double load the brush with the light mix and the dark mix. Blend on palette to soften color. With the light mix to the outside edge of the rose petals, apply strokes 1, 2, and 3.

Figure 4

Paint rose petal strokes 4, 5, 6, and 7.

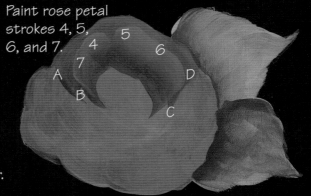

Apply a little extender to the leaf. Double load the brush with Fresh Foliage and Thicket + a touch of Burnt Umber. Paint the

Figure 5

Connect point B to point C, using a U stroke to form the base of the bowl of the rose. (Stroke 8)

Double load the brush with Fresh Foliage and Warm White. Stroke on the light side of the leaf.

Figure 6

Keeping the light mix to the outside edge of the rose petals, use comma strokes to paint petals 9, 10, 11, 12, and 13.

Quickly blend the colors on the leaf. Add more of any color, if desired. Let dry.

Figure 7

Connect point A to point D with a U stroke. (Stroke 14)

If needed, repaint, darken, or lighten the leaves.

Figure 8

Create petals over or on top of 9, 10, 11, 12 and 13. (Stroke 15 and 16)

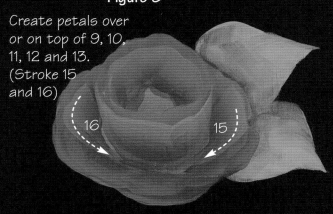

Figure 9

Fill in the center with scalloped strokes.

Figure 10

To finish the rose, add rolled S strokes and more comma strokes to create petals.

Roses for June
Red Roses Birthday Box

The technique for painting the red rose is the same as the pink or yellow rose – only the colors are different. I painted the red rose on the little birthday box, but any surface can be used.

SUPPLIES

Acrylic Enamels:

Berry Wine

Burnt Umber

Dioxazine Purple

Engine Red

Fresh Foliage

Pure Orange

Thicket

Warm White

Brushes:

Flats – #1, #2, #4, #8

Liner – #1

Surface:

Round china box, white with gold trim, 2" diameter

Other Supplies:

In addition to the basic painting supplies listed on page 14, you'll need:

Flow medium for acrylic enamels

Extender for acrylic enamels

Clear medium for acrylic enamels

Pattern can be found on page 75.

INSTRUCTIONS

See the Red Roses Painting Worksheet for detailed instructions for painting the flowers and leaves.

Prepare the Surface:
1. Wash the china box with soap and water. Rinse and dry thoroughly.
2. Wipe the surface with rubbing alcohol. Let dry.
3. Neatly trace the design on tracing paper and transfer with wax-free transfer paper.

Paint the Background:
1. Double load the #8 flat brush with Thicket and clear medium. Blend on the palette to soften the color. Apply around the outside edge of the design. Let dry thoroughly.
2. Apply a second coat to deepen the color if desired. Let dry.

Paint the Design:
Use the brush size that best fits the area you are painting. Allow paint to dry 20 to 30 minutes between coats.
1. Paint the leaves first. Paint leaves as shown on Red Roses Painting Worksheet. Because the leaves are under the roses, the rose petals will overlap the leaves.
2. Paint the roses as shown on Painting Worksheet.
3. Paint curlicues with the liner brush and Thicket thinned with flow medium.

Finish:
Let the birthday box air dry for 21 days *or* bake according to the paint manufacturer's instructions. ❏

Roses for June
Yellow Roses Birthday Box

The birthday boxes in this book are very small, so adjust your
brush size accordingly. I think you will enjoy painting roses,
and remember – no two roses will turn out the same!

SUPPLIES

Acrylic Enamels:

Burnt Sienna

Fresh Foliage

Lemon Custard

Thicket

Warm White

Brushes:

Flats – #2, #4, #10

Liner – #1

Surface:

Rectangular china box, white with
gold hinge, 2-1/2"

Other Supplies:

*In addition to the basic
painting supplies listed on
page 14, you'll need:*

Flow medium for acrylic
enamels

Extender for acrylic enamels

Clear medium for acrylic
enamels

*Pattern can be found
on page 75.*

INSTRUCTIONS

*See the Yellow Roses Painting Worksheet for detailed instructions for painting
the flowers and leaves.*

Prepare the Surface:
1. Wash the china box with soap and water. Rinse and dry thoroughly.
2. Wipe the surface with rubbing alcohol. Let dry.
3. Neatly trace the design on tracing paper and transfer with wax-free
   transfer paper.

Paint the Background:
1. Double load the #10 flat brush with Thicket and clear medium . Blend
   on the palette to soften the colors. Float around the outside edge of the
   design. Let dry 20 to 30 minutes.
2. Double load the #10 flat brush with Burnt Sienna and clear medium.
   Float in three different places over the Thicket.

Paint the Design:
*Use the brush size that best fits the area you are painting. Allow paint to dry 20
to 30 minutes between coats.*
1. Paint the leaves first. Paint leaves as shown on the Painting Worksheet.

Because the leaves are
under the roses, the rose
petals will overlap the
leaves.
2. Paint the roses as shown
   on the Painting Work-
   sheet.
3. Paint curlicues with the
   liner brush and Thicket
   thinned with flow medium.

Finish:
Let the birthday box air dry
for 21 days *or* bake according
to the paint manufacturer's
instructions. ❑

PALETTE OF COLORS

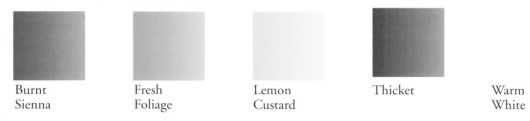

Burnt
Sienna

Fresh
Foliage

Lemon
Custard

Thicket

Warm
White

The roses in the step-by-step demonstration are much larger than the roses on the birthday box so that you can easily see the process.

Figure 1

Basecoat rose with Lemon Custard.
Basecoat leaves with two or three coats of
Fresh Foliage.

Figure 2

Basecoat rose with two
more coats of Lemon
Custard, drying
after each
coat.

Float s
base of
Thicket

Figure 3

Figure 4

Mix Lemon Custard + a
touch of Warm White to
lighten the yellow.

Apply extender to
the rose. Double
load the #2
flat brush with
Burnt Sienna
and the light yellow
mix. Paint strokes
4, 5, 6, and 7.

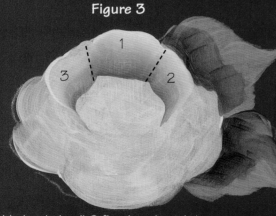

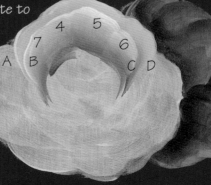

Double load the # 2 flat brush with Lemon
Custard and Burnt Sienna. Blend on palette
to soften color. Apply the first three strokes
to create the back petals of the rose.

Apply a little extender to one leaf at a time. While th
wet, reapply a little Burnt Sienna, then double load t
Fresh Foliage and Burnt Sienna and stroke in the da
leaf. Continue with Figures 6 and 7 while the extende

Figure 5

Connect point B to point C, using a U stroke to form the base of the bowl of the rose. (Stroke 8)

Figure 6

Double load the brush with Lemon Custard and Burnt Sienna. Paint strokes 9 and 10.

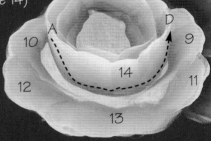

Working quickly, wipe the brush and double load with Fresh Foliage and Warm White. Stroke in the light areas of the leaf, pulling strokes from the edge toward the base.

Figure 7

Double load the brush with Lemon Custard and Burnt Sienna. Paint strokes 11, 12, and 13.

Working quickly while the extender is still wet, wipe the brush and blend from the base out and from the outside edge back toward the base. Let dry.

Figure 8

Double load the brush with the light yellow mix and Burnt Sienna. Blend on the palette so you have a full brush without excess paint on the edges of the brush. Stand the brush on the flat edge and paint a broken U stroke across the front of the rose, connecting point A to point D. (Stroke 14)

Scalloped strokes

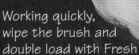

Figure 9

Paint small comma strokes to create fill-in petals.

Highlight leaf edges with tiny touches of Warm White.

Figure 10

Paint a rolled S stroke, connecting the outside edge of stroke 16 to the edge of stroke 14. You may choose another point on the rose at which to roll this stroke.

Double load the brush with the light yellow mix and Burnt Sienna. Paint scalloped strokes upward from the center.

Larkspur for July
Vase

Look at the background on this piece. It's gorgeous! Sponging combined with a striping technique makes this piece very dramatic. It takes some time to create, but it is well worth it — and it is easy to do (masking tape is the secret weapon).

SUPPLIES

Acrylic Enamels:

Dioxazine Purple

Fresh Foliage

Hauser Green Medium

Midnight

Pure Magenta

Thicket

Warm White

Brushes:

Filbert – #4

Flats – #2, #4, #6

Liner – #1, #10/0

Wash – 1"

Surface:

Chimney vase, cream, 7-1/2"

Other Supplies:

In addition to the basic painting supplies listed on page 14, you'll need:

Flow medium for acrylic enamels

Clear medium for acrylic enamels

Painters' tape

Scissors

Sea sponge

INSTRUCTIONS

See the Larkspur Painting Worksheet for detailed instructions for painting the flowers and leaves.

Prepare the Surface:

1. Wash the vase with soap and water. Rinse and dry thoroughly.
2. Wipe the surface with rubbing alcohol. Let dry.

Paint the Background:

1. Referring to the photograph, tape off the areas of the vase that will receive *no* background painting. Apply the tape in horizontal bands.

Pattern for Vase
Actual Size

2. Mix a wash for the background color – a very thin solution of Dioxazine Purple and flow medium.

3. Dip the sponge in water and squeeze it out thoroughly. Dip the sponge in the wash, then blot on a rag. Dab the purple wash on the vase, letting a lot of the background color show through. Let dry thoroughly.

4. Leaving the horizontal bands of tape in place, tape off vertical stripes at the top and bottom, using painter's tape.

5. Mix a second wash – a very thin solution of Pure Magenta and flow medium. Using the 1" wash brush, wash over the dried sponging to create the vertical stripes at top and bottom. Let dry.

6. Carefully remove the tape.

7. Neatly trace the design on tracing paper and transfer with wax-free transfer paper.

Paint the Design:
Use the brush size that best fits the area you are painting. Allow paint to dry 20 to 30 minutes between coats.

1. Paint the stems first as shown on Painting Worksheet. *See Fig. 1.* The flowers will be painted on top of the stems and the darkness of the paint will cover the green stems.

2. Add the Pure Magenta wash around the traced design. *See Fig. 2.*

3. Paint the flowers according to the Painting Worksheet.

4. Add bracts last.

Finish:
Let the vase air dry for 21 days *or* bake according to the paint manufacturer's instructions. ❏

Larkspur for July
Painting Worksheet

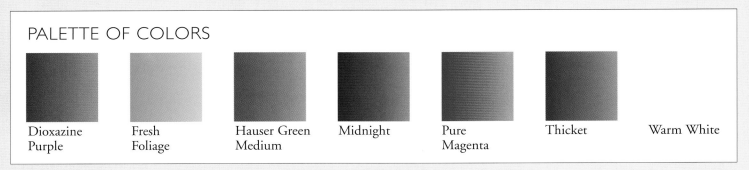

PALETTE OF COLORS

Dioxazine Purple   Fresh Foliage   Hauser Green Medium   Midnight   Pure Magenta   Thicket   Warm White

Figure 1

Thin Hauser Green Medium with flow medium. Using the #1 liner brush, paint stems and stocks. Let dry.

Shade with a little Thicket by going back over the lines.

Figure 2

Double load the 1" wash brush with Pure Magenta and clear medium. Keeping the Pure Magenta side of the brush next to the flowers, float the background around the design.

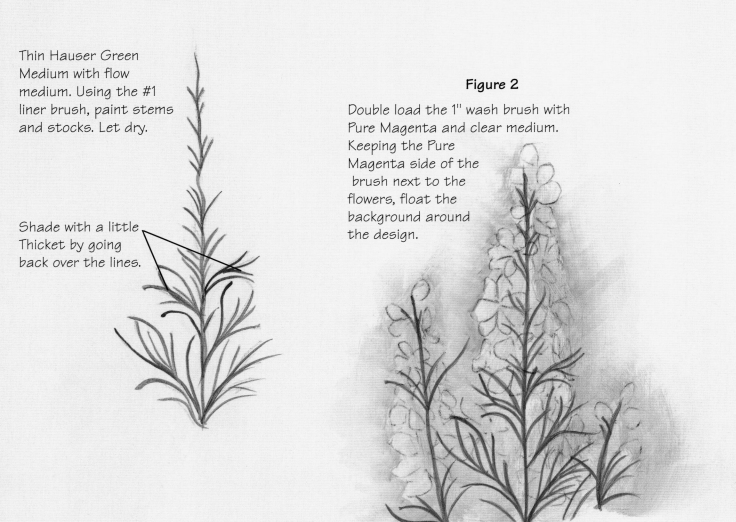

Figure 3

Using the #2 flat brush, stroke on the flower petals with Midnight.

Double load the 1" wash brush with Pure Magenta and clear medium. Keeping the Pure Magenta side of the brush next to the flowers, apply a second coat of background color around the basecoated flowers. It doesn't matter if the color overlaps a bit.

Figure 4

Load the #4 filbert brush with Pure Magenta. Stroke on the flowers.

Load the #4 filbert brush with Dioxazine Purple. Re-stroke the flowers.

Mix Dioxazine Purple + Midnight + Warm White (1:1:3). Using the #4 filbert brush, add high-lights by re-stroking the flower petals here and there.

Figure 5

Thin Fresh Foliage with flow medium. Using the #10/0 liner brush, make tiny dots in the centers of the most forward-facing flowers.

Using the #10/0 liner brush, highlight the flower centers with a few dots of Warm White.

Contrast is important – background flowers should be dark, and foreground flowers light.

— Create the bud bracts with the #1 liner brush and Fresh Foliage.

— Highlight bracts with Warm White.

Gladiola for August
Vase

Gladiolas are gorgeous in the garden and perfect for giving height to a stunning floral arrangement. Inexpensive plain vases can be made into heirloom pieces by adding some lovely floral designs.

SUPPLIES

Acrylic Enamels:

Fresh Foliage

Lemon Custard

Pure Orange

Thicket

Wicker White

Yellow Ochre

Brushes:

Flats – #4, #6, #8, #10, #12

Liner – #1

Surface:

Square porcelain vase, ash white, 7"

Other Supplies:

In addition to the basic painting supplies listed on page 14, you'll need:

Flow medium for acrylic enamels

Extender for acrylic enamels

Toothbrush for spattering

Pattern for Vase
Actual Size

INSTRUCTIONS

See the Gladiola Painting Worksheet for detailed instructions for painting the flowers and leaves.

Prepare the Surface:

1. Wash the vase with soap and water. Rinse and dry thoroughly.
2. Wipe the surface with rubbing alcohol. Let dry.
3. Neatly trace the design on tracing paper and transfer with wax-free transfer paper.

Paint the Design:

Use the brush size that best fits the area you are painting. Allow paint to dry 20 to 30 minutes between coats.

1. Paint the leaves of the gladiola first. Paint according to the instructions on the Painting Worksheet.
2. Paint the flowers, following the instructions on the Painting Worksheet.

Finish:

1. Spatter the project using the toothbrush and thinned Thicket.
2. Let the vase air dry for 21 days *or* bake according to the paint manufacturer's instructions. ❏

Gladiola for August
Painting Worksheet

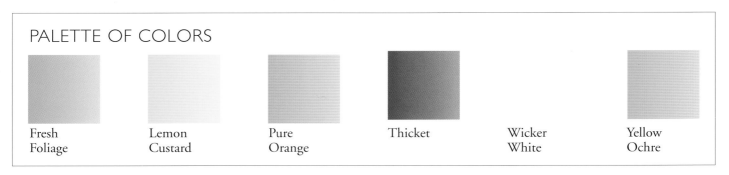

PALETTE OF COLORS

Fresh Foliage

Lemon Custard

Pure Orange

Thicket

Wicker White

Yellow Ochre

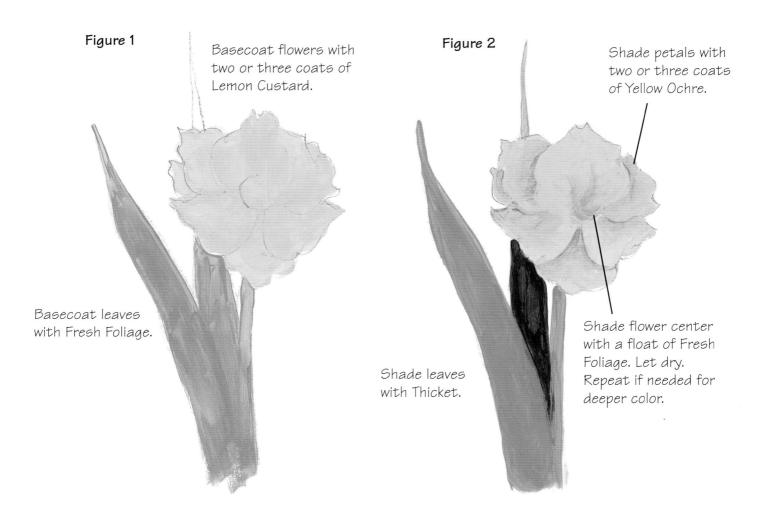

Figure 1

Basecoat flowers with two or three coats of Lemon Custard.

Basecoat leaves with Fresh Foliage.

Figure 2

Shade petals with two or three coats of Yellow Ochre.

Shade leaves with Thicket.

Shade flower center with a float of Fresh Foliage. Let dry. Repeat if needed for deeper color.

Figure 3

Highlight flower petals with floats of Wicker White. Float on the outside edges of the petals, then pull it in toward the center.

Figure 4

Highlight petals again with floats of Wicker White.

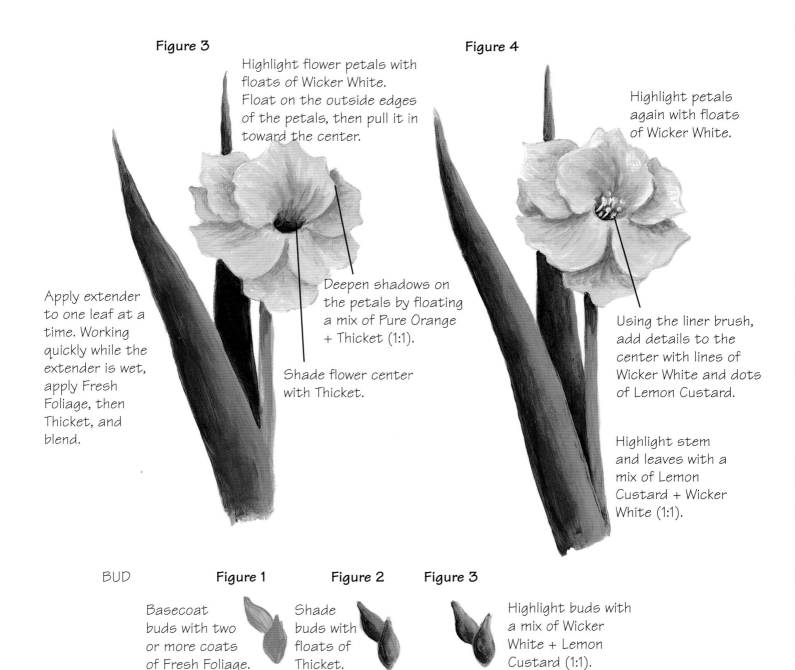

Apply extender to one leaf at a time. Working quickly while the extender is wet, apply Fresh Foliage, then Thicket, and blend.

Deepen shadows on the petals by floating a mix of Pure Orange + Thicket (1:1).

Shade flower center with Thicket.

Using the liner brush, add details to the center with lines of Wicker White and dots of Lemon Custard.

Highlight stem and leaves with a mix of Lemon Custard + Wicker White (1:1).

BUD

Figure 1

Basecoat buds with two or more coats of Fresh Foliage.

Figure 2

Shade buds with floats of Thicket.

Figure 3

Highlight buds with a mix of Wicker White + Lemon Custard (1:1).

OPENING BUD

Figure 1

Basecoat petals with two or three coats of Lemon Custard.

Figure 2

Figure 3

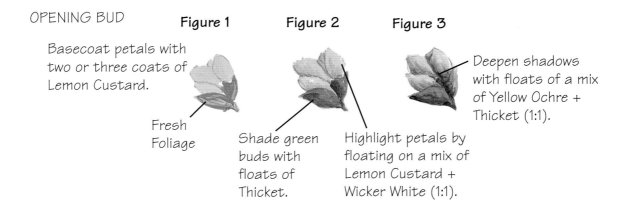

Fresh Foliage

Shade green buds with floats of Thicket.

Highlight petals by floating on a mix of Lemon Custard + Wicker White (1:1).

Deepen shadows with floats of a mix of Yellow Ochre + Thicket (1:1).

Morning Glories for September
Bud Vase

There isn't anything more gentle or more blue than a morning glory.
They are not difficult to paint – just a little shading gives the
trumpet center its dimension. The design for this piece of porcelain
paints relatively quickly and makes an elegant gift.

SUPPLIES

Acrylic Enamels:

Azure Blue

Fresh Foliage

Hauser Green Medium

Lemon Custard

Pure Magenta

Thicket

Wicker White

Brushes:

Flats – #4, #8, #10

Liner – #1

Wash – 1"

Surface:

Porcelain bud vase, soft blue, 7"

Other Supplies:

*In addition to the basic painting
supplies listed on page 14,
you'll need:*

Flow medium for acrylic enamels

Clear medium for acrylic enamels

Optional: Extender for acrylic
   enamels

Fine sandpaper

INSTRUCTIONS

*See the Morning Glories Painting Worksheet for detailed instructions for
painting the flowers and leaves.*

Prepare the Surface:
1. Lightly sand the porcelain surface.
2. Wipe the surface with rubbing alcohol. Let dry.
3. Neatly trace the design on tracing paper and transfer with wax-free transfer paper.

*The morning glories on this cup and saucer were painted with the same technique as
the morning glories on the vase. They are smaller so you will need to choose smaller
brushes.*

Paint the Background:

1. Double load the 1" wash brush with Azure Blue and flow medium. Blend on the palette to soften the color. Keeping the blue side of the brush against the flowers and leaves, float around the outside edge of the design. Let dry. *See Figure 1.*

2. Double load the 1" wash brush with Pure Magenta and flow medium. Blend on the palette to soften the color. Keeping the magenta side of the brush against the flowers and leaves, float under the trumpet area of the petals and at the base of the flower. *See Figure 2.* Let dry.

Paint the Design:

Use the brush size that best fits the area you are painting. Allow paint to dry 20 to 30 minutes between coats.

1. Paint the leaves first. Paint according to the instructions on the Painting Worksheet.

2. Paint the flower next, painting as shown on Painting Worksheet.

3. Paint the bracts at the base of the flowers last.

4. Paint vines and curlicues using the liner brush and Hauser Green Medium thinned with flow medium.

Finish:

Let the vase air dry for 21 days *or* bake according to the paint manufacturer's instructions. ❏

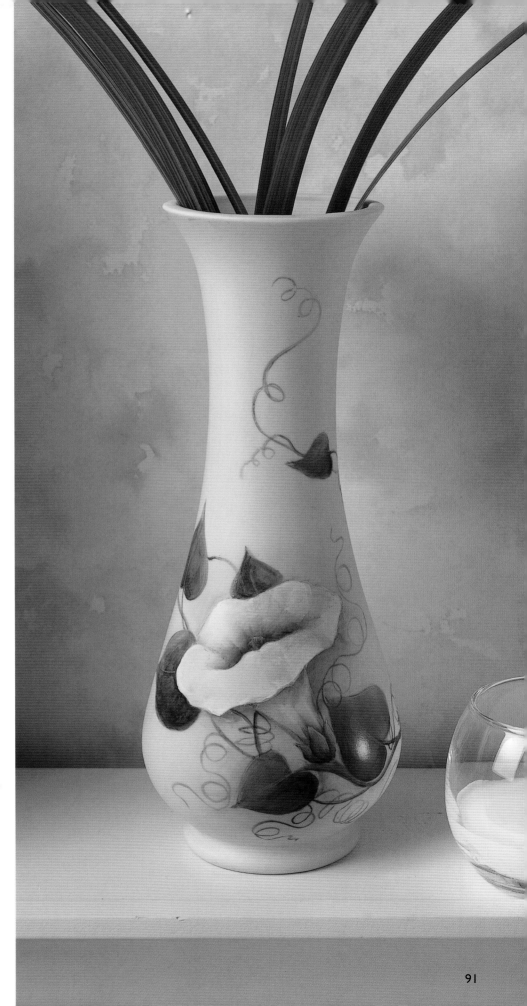

Morning Glories for September
Painting Worksheet

PALETTE OF COLORS

 Azure Blue

 Fresh Foliage

 Hauser Green Medium

Lemon Custard

 Pure Magenta

 Thicket

Wicker White

Figure 1

Float background with Azure Blue and flow medium.

Using the #4 flat brush, Basecoat leaves and bracts with two coats of Hauser Green Medium.

Figure 2

Float background in three places with Pure Magenta and flow medium.

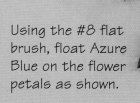

Using the #8 flat brush, float Azure Blue on the flower petals as shown.

Figure 3

Deepen shading on flower with floats of Pure Magenta.

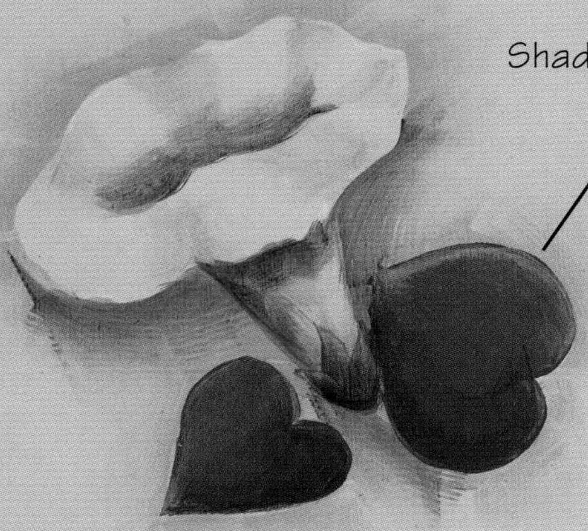

Shade leaves with a float of Thicket.

Highlight leaves with a float of Fresh Foliage.

Repeat shading and highlighting on leaves to strengthen the color.

Figure 4

Highlight edges of the flower with a float of Wicker White.

Figure 5

Add a touch of Lemon Custard to create the center. Let dry and apply a second coat, keeping it soft.

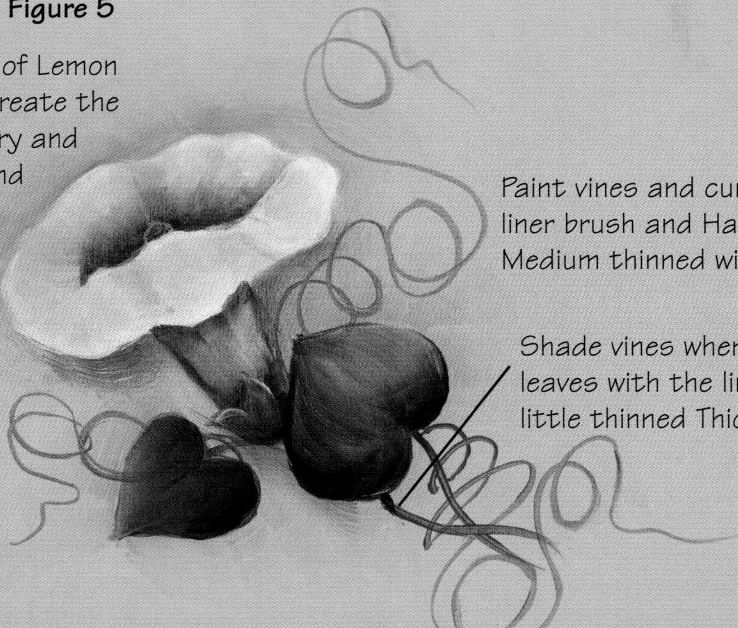

Paint vines and curlicues with the liner brush and Hauser Green Medium thinned with flow medium.

Shade vines where they go behind leaves with the liner brush and a little thinned Thicket.

Morning Glories
for September

Pattern for Bud Vase
Actual Size

Pattern for Cup
& Saucer
Actual Size

Bonus
Pattern

Marigold for October
Glass Bottle

I'll bet you have an old or new glass bottle around that was too cool to part with. Bring it out and paint it. That is what I did. No one knew it had belonged to my mother. Using a painted bottle for dishwashing liquid will add charm to your sink. Or use it to serve olive oil for dipping; or for serving salad dressing. Did you know that the Marigold is also called a calendula?

SUPPLIES

Acrylic Enamels:

Dioxazine Purple

Fresh Foliage

Hunter Green

Lemon Custard

Pure Orange

Wicker White

Brushes:

Flats – #2, #4, #6, #8

Liner – #1

Surface:

Glass bottle or jar

Other Supplies:

In addition to the basic painting supplies listed on page 14, you'll need:

Optional: Extender for acrylic enamels

INSTRUCTIONS

See the Marigold Painting Worksheet for detailed instructions for painting the flowers and leaves.

Prepare the Surface:
1. Wash the bottle or jar with soap and water. Rinse and dry thoroughly.
2. Wipe the surface with rubbing alcohol. Let dry.
3. Neatly trace the design on tracing paper and transfer with wax-free transfer paper.

Paint the Design:
Use the brush size that best fits the area you are painting. Allow paint to dry 20 to 30 minutes between coats.
1. If you paint the design on a dark surface you will need to undercoat the complete design with Wicker White. *See Fig. 1.* Allow White to dry thoroughly before painting marigold.
2. Paint the leaves of the marigold first. Following instructions and steps as shown on Painting Worksheet.
3. Paint the petals of the marigold next. Following Painting Worksheet.

Finish:
Let the bottle or jar air dry for 21 days *or* bake according to the paint manufacturer's instructions. Trim with raffia or ribbons. ❏

Pattern for Bottle
Actual Size

Marigold for October
Painting Worksheet

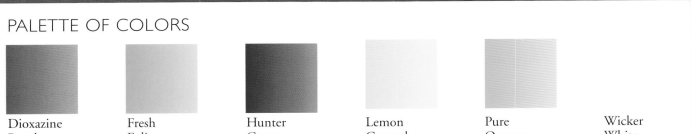

PALETTE OF COLORS

Dioxazine Purple

Fresh Foliage

Hunter Green

Lemon Custard

Pure Orange

Wicker White

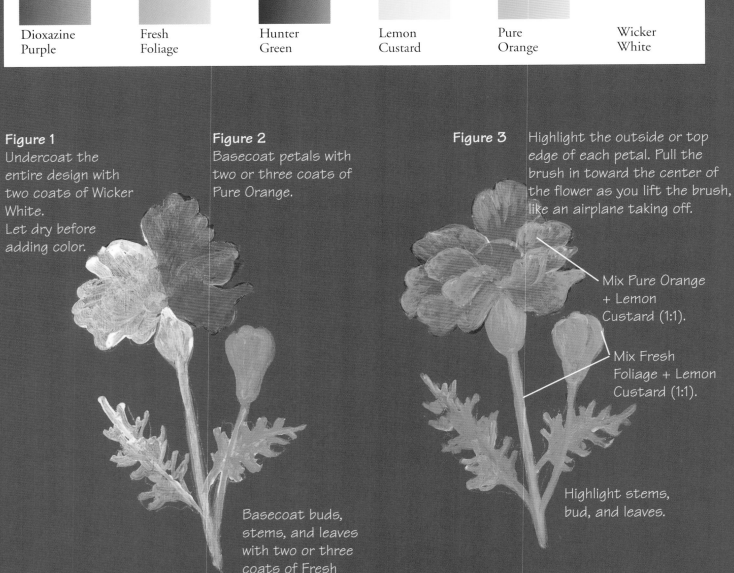

Figure 1
Undercoat the entire design with two coats of Wicker White.
Let dry before adding color.

Figure 2
Basecoat petals with two or three coats of Pure Orange.

Basecoat buds, stems, and leaves with two or three coats of Fresh Foliage.

Figure 3 Highlight the outside or top edge of each petal. Pull the brush in toward the center of the flower as you lift the brush, like an airplane taking off.

Mix Pure Orange + Lemon Custard (1:1).

Mix Fresh Foliage + Lemon Custard (1:1).

Highlight stems, bud, and leaves.

Figure 4

Mix Dioxazine Purple + Pure Orange (1:1).

Float shading at the base of each petal.

Figure 5

Shade the base of each petal again with the Dioxazine Purple + Pure Orange mixture to deepen shading.

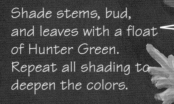

Shade stems, bud, and leaves with a float of Hunter Green. Repeat all shading to deepen the colors.

Highlight the opposite side of leaves and stems with Lemon Custard.

Figure 6

Shade the center of the flower with the Dioxazine Purple + Pure Orange mix.

Highlight outside edges of petals with the liner brush and Lemon Custard.

Darken the left side of stems with an unequal mix of Hunter Green + a little Dioxazine Purple.

Figure 7

Paint the center with the liner brush and a brush mix of Lemon Custard + Pure Orange. Layer short strokes on top of each other. Next add strokes of just Pure Orange. Then add a layer of strokes of Pure Orange + Dioxazine Purple.

Add a tiny touch of Fresh Foliage to a little Lemon Custard. Highlight stems, bud, and leaves.

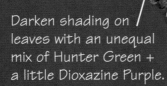

Darken shading on leaves with an unequal mix of Hunter Green + a little Dioxazine Purple.

Chrysanthemum for November
Vase

This is a favorite of mine. I seldom paint anything this large, but I couldn't resist
this hunter green porcelain. It is so rich with the golden chrysanthemums.

SUPPLIES

Acrylic Enamels:

Autumn Leaves

Burnt Sienna

Fresh Foliage

Metallic Gold

Hauser Green Medium

Pure Orange

School Bus Yellow

Warm White

Brushes:

Flats – #4, #8, #16, #20

Liner – #1

Round – #5

Surface:

Vase, hunter green, 18" tall

Other Supplies:

*In addition to the basic painting
supplies listed on page 14, you'll
need:*

Flow medium for acrylic enamels

Extender for acrylic enamels

Dauber

Toothbrush for spattering

INSTRUCTIONS

*See the Chrysanthemum Painting Worksheet for detailed instructions for paint-
ing the flowers and leaves.*

Prepare the Surface:

1. Wash the vase with soap and water. Rinse and dry thoroughly.
2. Wipe the surface with rubbing alcohol. Let dry.
3. Neatly trace the design on tracing paper and transfer with wax-free
   transfer paper.

PRISCILLA'S TIPS FOR PAINTING CHRYSANTHEMUMS

• Study the pattern. I have divided the chrysanthemum in two
sections. The upper portion is a ball with an X at the bottom. The
lower portion is comma strokes that draw to the X. Paint the upper
portion or ball first, then turn the flower upside down and paint the
lower portion, pulling the comma strokes in toward the X at the
base of the ball.

• It is important to let this flower
breathe. Let some of the background color show through.
Don't paint it as a solid mass of
strokes.

• If you don't like what you paint,
use a damp rag and wipe from
the outside edge in toward the
center to remove the strokes,
and start again.

Paint the Design:

Use the brush size that best fits the area you are painting. Allow paint to dry 20 to 30 minutes between coats.

1. I didn't undercoat this design even though I was painting on a dark surface. I used the dark surface to help shadow and add depth to the painting. Add the light highlighting to the leaves first as shown in *Fig. 1*.

2. Paint all the leaves first, following the instructions on the Painting Worksheet.

3. Paint the flowers next, following the Painting Worksheet.

4. Paint stems with Hauser Green Medium. Shade with Thicket.

5. Thin Hauser Green Medium with flow medium. Using the #1 liner brush, slowly paint the curlicues.

Finish:

1. Spatter the vase lightly with Metallic Gold.

2. Apply Metallic Gold around the top rim of the vase using a dauber.

3. Let the vase air dry for 21 days *or* bake according to the paint manufacturer's instructions. ❏

Chrysanthemum for November
Painting Worksheet

PALETTE OF COLORS

Autumn Leaves

Burnt Sienna

Fresh Foliage

Metallic Gold

Hauser Green Medium

Pure Orange

School Bus Yellow

Warm White

Wicker White

Figure 1

Double load the brush with Thicket and Hauser Green Medium. Blend on palette to soften color. Apply shadow at base of leaf.

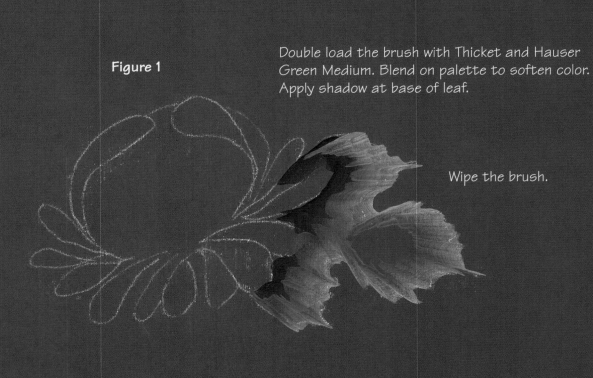

Wipe the brush.

Double load with Hauser Green Medium and Warm White. Keep the Warm White to the outside as you scribble, by moving the brush slowly back and forth, to create the jagged edges of the leaf.

For lighter leaves, use Fresh Foliage in place of Hauser Green Medium.

Figure 2

Rough in the flower shape with loose strokes of School Bus Yellow, Pure Orange, Autumn Leaves, and Burnt Sienna . Let dry.

To vary the colors of the chrysanthemums, use more yellow on some, more orange on others.

Apply a little extender to the leaf. While the extender is wet, wipe the brush and pick up more Hauser Green Medium and Thicket.

Apply the Thicket to the base of the leaf. Wipe the brush and blend. Add more of any colors needed to tie the leaf together.

Figure 3

Work quickly while the extender is wet, so the colors will bleed through from beneath.

Fill the #5 round brush with Warm White. Beginning with the upper part of the flower, paint comma strokes, drawing the strokes toward the X.

Apply extender to the flower and reapply the colors.

Blend leaf colors while the extender is wet.

To paint the lower part of the flower, turn the piece upside down. Draw the comma strokes toward the X.

Figure 4

Continue adding petals as needed.

Highlight leaf edges with Warm White, pulling strokes back into the leaf.

Chrysanthemum for November

Pattern for Vase

Enlarge @165% for actual size.

Chrysanthemum for November
Plate

This simple plate shows off the subtle color variations in the chrysanthemums. You can easily create your own arrangements and colors when you understand the basics of painting these gorgeous autumn flowers.

INSTRUCTIONS

The design was painted on a 12" frosted glass plate. You can use this plate as a charger, placing a clear glass plate or plain white smaller plate on top of it for serving.

Use the same color palette as used for the Chrysanthemum Vase project. The flower will look a little different without the dark background behind it.

Pattern for Plate

Enlarge @130% for actual size.

Holly for December
Dinner Set

A beautiful set for holiday entertaining, and not at all hard to paint. Build a set for yourself or a special friend by painting a place setting each year as a gift. Don't need a set? Paint a cookie dish or a cocoa mug!

SUPPLIES

Acrylic Enamels:

Berry Wine

Burnt Umber

Cobalt

Engine Red

Fresh Foliage

Hauser Green Medium

Pure Orange

Thicket

Wicker White

Brushes:

Flats – #2, #4, #8, #10, #12

Liner – #1

Surfaces:

White china place setting

Other Supplies:

In addition to the basic painting supplies listed on page 14, you'll need:

Flow medium for acrylic enamels

Pictured right: A close-up view of plate design.

INSTRUCTIONS

See the Holly Painting Worksheet for detailed instructions for painting the flowers and leaves.

Do not paint surfaces that will come in contact with food.

Prepare the Surfaces:
1. Wash the china pieces with soap and water. Rinse and dry thoroughly.
2. Wipe the surfaces with rubbing alcohol. Let dry.
3. Neatly trace the design on tracing paper and transfer with wax-free transfer paper.
4. Mix this color:
   Ice Blue Mix – Wicker White + a touch of Cobalt + a touch of Burnt Umber + a touch of Thicket (1:T:T:T)

Paint the Design:
Use the brush size that best fits the area you are painting. Allow paint to dry 20 to 30 minutes between coats.
1. Paint the holly leaves first, following the instructions on the Painting Worksheet.

2. Paint the ribbon next, following the instructions on the Painting Worksheet.

3. Paint the berries last, following the instructions on the Painting Worksheet.

4. Paint curlicues with the #1 liner brush and a mix of Thicket + Fresh Foliage (1:1), thinned with flow medium.

Finish:

Let the pieces air dry for 21 days *or* bake according to the paint manufacturer's instructions. ❑

Holly for December
Painting Worksheet

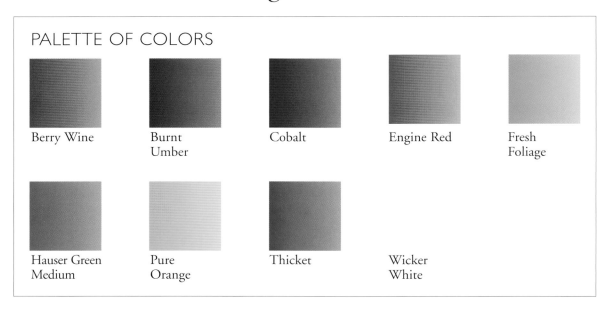

PALETTE OF COLORS

Berry Wine

Burnt Umber

Cobalt

Engine Red

Fresh Foliage

Hauser Green Medium

Pure Orange

Thicket

Wicker White

Figure 1

Basecoat leaves with two or three coats of Hauser Green Medium.

Figure 2

Shade leaves with a float of Thicket. Let dry. Repeat to deepen the color.

Basecoat the ribbon with Engine Red. Let dry. Repeat two or three times.

Figure 3

Shade the ribbon with a float of Berry Wine. Let dry. Repeat as many times as desired to deepen the color.

Highlight leaves with a float of Ice Blue Mix.

Basecoat berries with Engine Red. Let dry. Apply two or three more coats, drying after each coat.

Figure 4

Vein the leaves with a float of Thicket and flow medium. Let dry. Repeat the veining.

Highlight the ribbon with two or three coats of Pure Orange.

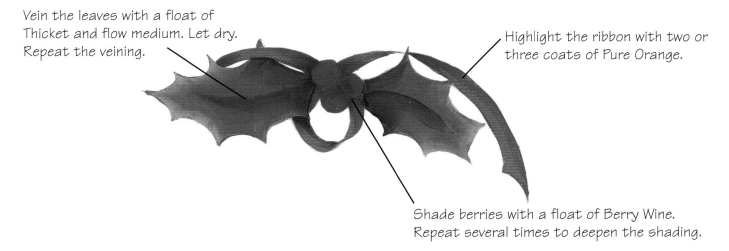

Shade berries with a float of Berry Wine. Repeat several times to deepen the shading.

Figure 5

Highlight berries with a float of Pure Orange. Repeat.

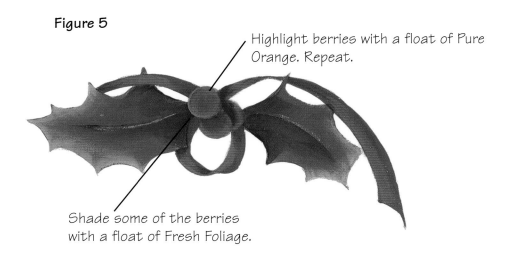

Shade some of the berries with a float of Fresh Foliage.

Holly for December

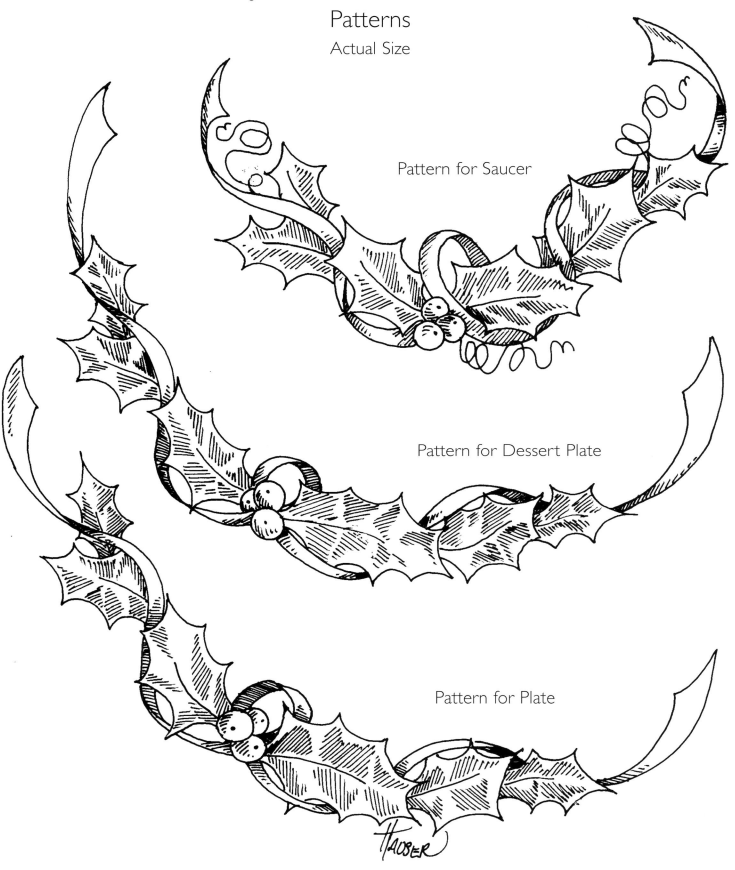

Patterns

Actual Size

Pattern for Saucer

Pattern for Dessert Plate

Pattern for Plate

HAUSER

Pattern for Cup

Pattern for Bowl

Nest & Eggs
Moon Vase

Look at this moon vase — isn't it stunning? And it's so much
fun to paint! The round shape of the vase, in contrast
with the gingham-like stripes makes it very dramatic.

SUPPLIES

Acrylic Enamels:

Burnt Sienna

Burnt Umber

Fresh Foliage

Hauser Green Medium

Lemon Custard

Midnight

Pure Magenta

Thicket

Warm White

Yellow Ochre

Brushes:

Flats – #2, #4, #6, #8, #10, #12

Liner – #1

Wash – 1"

Surface:

Moon vase, white, 9" diameter

Other Supplies:

*In addition to the basic painting
supplies listed on page 14,
you'll need:*

Flow medium for acrylic enamels

Extender for acrylic enamels

Toothbrush for spattering

INSTRUCTIONS

*See the Nest & Eggs Painting Worksheet for detailed instructions for painting
the flowers and leaves.*

Prepare the Surface:

1. Wash the vase with soap and water. Rinse and dry thoroughly.
2. Wipe the surface with rubbing alcohol. Let dry.

Paint the Gingham Background:

*Practice on the back of the vase. You can remove your practice strokes by scrubbing
with alcohol. Once you feel comfortable, paint the gingham on the front. Don't
try to be perfect – this is hand painted, and this is the way you want it to be.*

1. Thin Fresh Foliage with flow medium. Using the #8 flat brush, paint
   evenly spaced vertical lines from top to bottom of the vase. Let dry 20 to
   30 minutes.
2. Using the same brush and thinned Fresh Foliage, paint evenly spaced
   horizontal lines. Let dry 20 to 30 minutes.
3. Neatly trace the design on tracing paper and transfer with wax-free
   transfer paper.

Paint the Design:

*Use the brush size that best fits the area you are painting. Allow paint to dry 20
to 30 minutes between coats.*

1. Shade around the traced design first, following *Figures 1 and 2* on the
   Painting Worksheet.
2. Paint the leaves, then the nest, then the branches. Following the Painting
   Worksheet for instructions and steps.
3. Paint curlicues with the #1 liner brush and Thicket thinned with flow
   medium.

Finish:

Let the vase air dry for 21 days *or* bake according to the paint manufacturer's instructions. ❏

Pattern can be found on page 121.

Nest & Eggs
Painting Worksheet

PALETTE OF COLORS

Burnt Sienna

Burnt Umber

Fresh Foliage

Hauser Green Medium

Lemon Custard

Midnight

Pure Magenta

Thicket

Warm White

Yellow Ochre

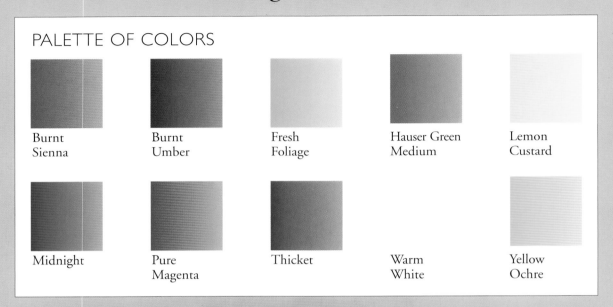

Figure 1

Double load the 1" wash brush with Thicket and flow medium. Blend on palette to soften color. Keeping the Thicket toward the design, wash around the design.

Using the #6 or #8 flat brush, undercoat the eggs with Warm White. Let dry. Repeat three times.

Basecoat the branch with a small flat brush and Burnt Umber. Let dry. Repeat three times.

Basecoat the nest with six coats of Yellow Ochre, drying after each coat.

Using the #8 or #10 flat brush, basecoat leaves with Fresh Foliage. Let dry. Repeat three times.

Figure 2

Double load the 1" wash brush with Burnt Sienna and flow medium. Add touches around the design.

Shade the eggs with a float of Midnight.

Shade the nest with a float of Burnt Umber.

Shade the branch with a float of Burnt Umber.

Shade the leaves with a float of Thicket.

Deepen shadings with additional coats. Allow the paint to dry 20 to 30 minutes between coats.

Figure 3

Thin Yellow Ochre, Burnt Umber, and Warm White with flow medium. Using the liner brush, make curvy lines to begin building the straw.

Shade the branch with a float of Burnt Umber.

Highlight the branch with a float of Warm White.

Apply extender to one leaf at a time.

Double load the brush with Hauser Green Medium and Thicket. Stroke on the dark side of the leaf.

Wipe the brush.

Double load with Hauser Green Medium and Warm White. Stroke on the light side of the leaf.

Working quickly while the extender is wet, continue with Steps 4 and 5.

Figure 4

Continue building the nest with liner brush strokes of Burnt Umber, Yellow Ochre, and Warm White.

Cover everything except the area of the eggs with paper towels. Using a toothbrush, spatter the eggs with thinned Pure Magenta. Leave covering in place.

Add a touch of Lemon Custard in the center of the leaf.

Figure 5

Using a toothbrush, spatter the eggs with a little thinned Midnight.

Wipe the brush and blend leaves lightly. Let dry.

Deepen shading on leaves if needed.

Double load the 1" wash brush with Lemon Custard and flow medium. Add touches of yellow here and there around the design, over the Thicket and Burnt Umber.

Complete the nest with liner brush strokes of Burnt Umber, Yellow Ochre, and Warm White.

Honey Bees
Ginger Jar

I have always loved to paint bees on a black background. They
really pop! This is a great design for brightening up a kitchen. I love
to paint these bees on honey jars and give to friends as gifts.

SUPPLIES

Acrylic Enamels:

Coffee Bean

Licorice

Lemon Custard

Wicker White

Brushes:

Flat – #10

Liner – #1

Surface:

Ginger jar, black

Other Supplies:

*In addition to the basic painting
supplies listed on page 14, you'll
need:*

Flow medium for acrylic enamels

Sponge dauber, 5/8"

Chalk

INSTRUCTIONS

*See the Honey Bees Painting Worksheet for detailed instructions for painting the
flowers and leaves.*

Prepare the Surface:
1. Wash the ginger jar with soap and water. Rinse and dry thoroughly.
2. Wipe the surface with rubbing alcohol. Let dry.
3. Trace patterns then transfer patterns with white chalk to the jar.

Paint the Design:
Follow the Painting Worksheet for instructions for painting the bees.

Trim the Jar:
1. Paint the trim areas with several coats of Lemon Custard. Let dry 20 to
   30 minutes after each coat.
2. Antique the Lemon Custard areas using a #10 flat brush double loaded
   with Coffee Bean and flow medium.

Finish:
Let the vase air dry for 21 days *or* bake according to the paint manufacturer's instructions. ❏

Pattern can be found on page 121.

Honey Bees
Painting Worksheet

PALETTE OF COLORS

Coffee
Bean

Lemon
Custard

Licorice

Wicker
White

Figure 1

Double load a 5/8" dauber with Lemon Custard and Coffee Bean. Load the dauber full of paint, then blot on a rag. Keeping the darker color to the left, make a half circle for the upper body — touch, press, wiggle, and lift. Repeat if needed.

Figure 2

Pick up more paint. Make a second circle overlapping the first. Keep the darker color to the left. Wipe the dauber.

Figure 3

Pick up a small amount of Licorice on the edge. Apply to the top and bottom of the second section.

Figure 4

Paint the head with a #1 liner brush and a gray mix of Licorice + Wicker White (1:1).

Figure 5

Using the liner brush and Licorice thinned with flow medium, paint the stripes. Each stripe is a series of tiny strokes.

Figure 6

Using the liner brush, paint the legs with the gray mix, thinned with flow medium.

Figure 7

Double load a #10 flat brush with Wicker White and flow medium. Blend on palette to soften color. Keeping the white to the outside, paint the wings.

Honey Bees

Pattern
Actual Size

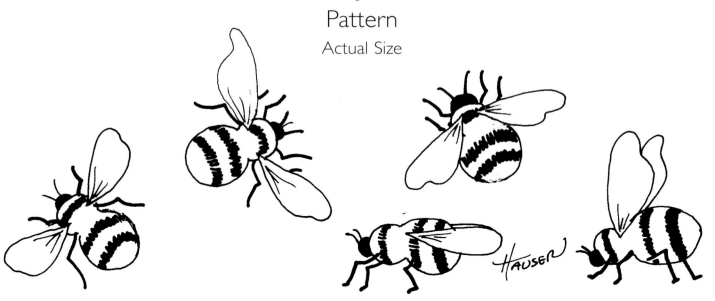

Nest & Eggs

Pattern
Actual Size

Instructions are on page 114.

Trailing Ivy
Ginger Jar Canister

SUPPLIES

Acrylic Enamels:

See "Palette of Colors"

Brushes:

Flats – #4, #6, #8

Liner – #1

Toothbrush for spattering

PALETTE OF COLORS

Fresh
Foliage

Thicket

Warm
White

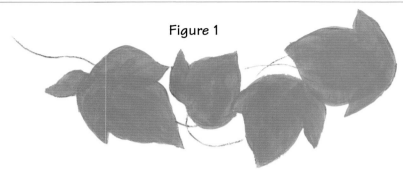

Figure 1

Using a #4 flat brush, basecoat leaves and stems with Fresh Foliage. Let dry. Repeat two or three times, drying 20 to 30 minutes after each coat.

Double load a #8 flat brush with Thicket and flow medium. Blend on palette to soften color. Shade the bases of the leaves. Let dry 20 to 30 minutes. Repeat two or three times to deepen the color.

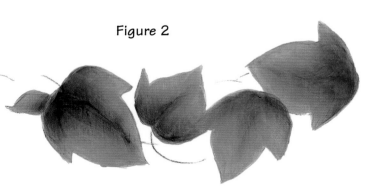

Figure 2

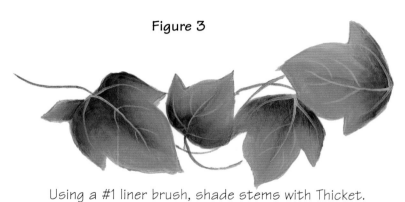

Figure 3

Double load the #8 flat brush with Warm White and flow medium. Highlight the light sides of the leaves.

Mix Fresh Foliage + Warm White (1:1), and thin with extender. Stroke leaf veins with the liner brush.

Using a #1 liner brush, shade stems with Thicket.

INSTRUCTIONS

Paint the Design:
Paint the ivy on the ginger jar according to the Painting Worksheet.

Finish:
1. Paint curlicues with the #1 liner brush and Fresh Foliage thinned with flow medium. Shade curlicues with Thicket.
2. Using a toothbrush, spatter with Thicket that has been thinned with a little extender.
3. Paint trim on the lid with two or three coats of Thicket.
4. Let the jar and lid air dry for 21 days *or* bake according to the paint manufacturer's instructions.

Patterns

Butterflies & Moths

Patterns for Stencils

Instructions are on page 29.

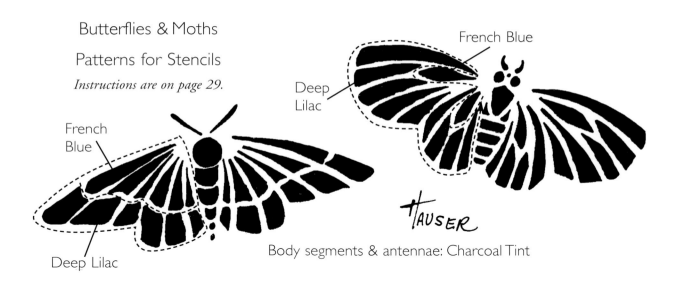

French Blue

Deep Lilac

French Blue

Deep Lilac

Body segments & antennae: Charcoal Tint

Trailing Ivy
Pattern for Ginger Jar Canister
Actual Size

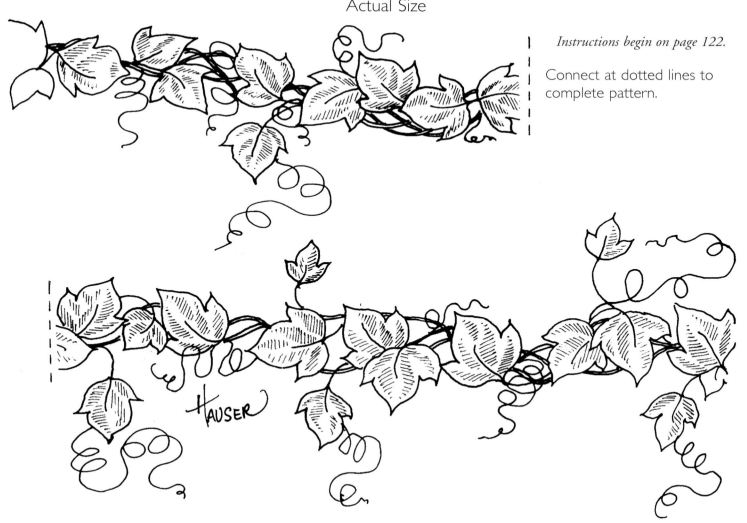

Instructions begin on page 122.

Connect at dotted lines to complete pattern.

Stripes, Dots & Linework

Pattern for Teapot & Cups

Actual Size

Instructions are on page 36.

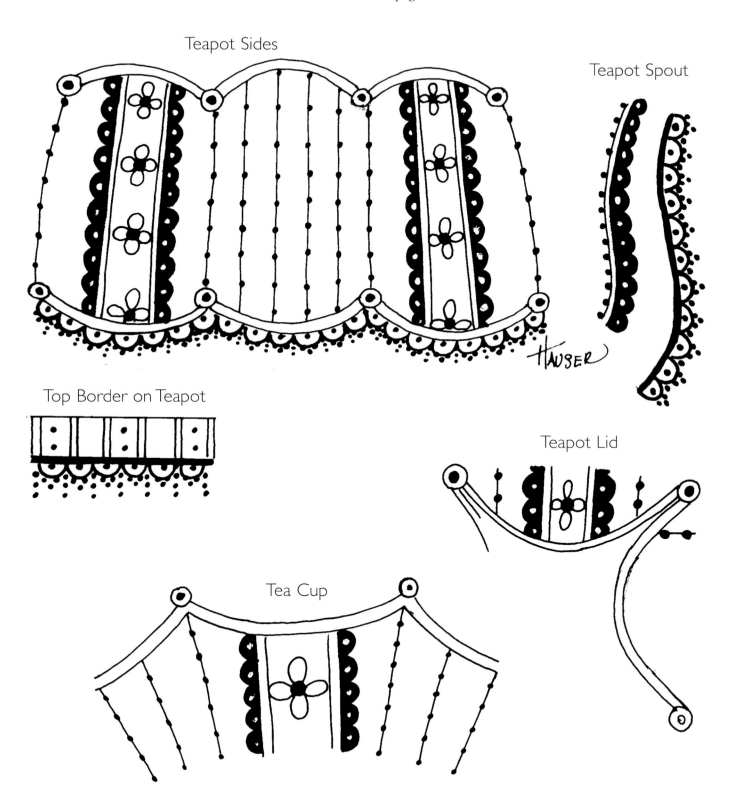

Teapot Sides

Teapot Spout

Top Border on Teapot

Teapot Lid

Tea Cup

Metric Conversion Chart

Inches to Millimeters and Centimeters

Inches	MM	CM
1/8	3	.3
1/4	6	.6
3/8	10	1.0
1/2	13	1.3
5/8	16	1.6
3/4	19	1.9
7/8	22	2.2
1	25	2.5
1-1/4	32	3.2
1-1/2	38	3.8
1-3/4	44	4.4
2	51	5.1
3	76	7.6
4	102	10.2
5	127	12.7
6	152	15.2
7	178	17.8
8	203	20.3
9	229	22.9
10	254	25.4
11	279	27.9
12	305	30.5

Yards to Meters

Yards	Meters
1/8	.11
1/4	.23
3/8	.34
1/2	.46
5/8	.57
3/4	.69
7/8	.80
1	.91
2	1.83
3	2.74
4	3.66
5	4.57
6	5.49
7	6.40
8	7.32
9	8.23
10	9.14

Index

Continued on next page